In Their Own Voice:

Intercultural Meaning in Everyday Stories

Anne P. Copeland

and

Marissa Lombardi

with members of the International Writers' Club

The Interchange Institute

The Interchange Institute
tel (617) 566-2227
www.interchangeinstitute.org
writers@interchangeinstitute.org

Individual authors in this collection have given their permission for their stories to be in a volume published by The Interchange Institute, a non-profit organization, with the assurance that all proceeds from the collection will go to support people in intercultural transition, the mission of the Institute. Authors were always welcome to submit stories to the Club anonymously (an option that a few have chosen) or for discussion but not publication.

Library of Congress Control Number: 2011924433
ISBN: 978-1974670727

Acknowledgements

I am deeply grateful to and wholly in awe of the 100+ members of the International Writers' Club who have participated over the years. They made my job easy, by clearly describing their experience in a thoughtful, respectful way. Surely, surely some of the things they observed must have made them frustrated or angry, but their stories were always polite, inquisitive, and open to a new perspective. All the writers put their lives and careers on hold so they could help move their families halfway around the world. Most did this for their spouses' careers, but also for themselves and their children – to learn English and to see what life in a multicultural community could be like. As mentors to their children, they are the tenders of the world's new global citizens. We are in good hands with them.

– Anne Copeland

Table of Contents

Cultural Adaptation

Customs

Education

Dimension Descriptions

Appendix

Indexes

Introduction

The stories you hold in your hand are a treasure for anyone interested in understanding intercultural transition. In the authentic, personal, everyday moments portrayed here, we gain precious access to the thinking and action behind the value differences that reveal themselves at work and in our daily lives. The writers describe the universal experience of those who find themselves in a new country, looking both forward and backward, as they navigate a barrage of new experiences and beliefs.

In the rest of our work as interculturalists, we read and teach and train about cultural differences. We conduct research on families and individuals who live and work in new countries. And we explain and explore classic concepts of cultural values and beliefs to students, members of multicultural groups, and those moving to new countries. In short, we have theory, research, and official definitions at our fingertips. But we think the stories from The International Writers' Club do more to illustrate what it's really like to live in the space between cultures than any other resource we have to offer.

On the surface, many of these stories are about what happens between a mother and a young child in a school classroom or neighborhood, so if you work with students or adults you may wonder if they're for you. But this is exactly where cultural differences in values and attitudes are formed – in the early family and school environment that supports children and prepares them to work within the value system of their culture. Nobody thinks cultural differences are in-born; so where and how are they learned? What do parents of young children actually say and do that makes their children value collectivism as opposed to individualism? What values are teachers trying to instill in their students, as preparation for success in their culture – and how do they actually do it? It is in the countless daily responses to homework, birthday parties, neighbors, shopkeepers, and waitresses that children absorb the implicit messages about what their family and culture values. It is one thing to memorize a list of cultural differences, but quite another, richer thing to understand how they were created, and to see with clarity how these values all fit together. These stories are a window into that process of cultural value formation.

In these stories, we also get a clear narration from expatriates navigating a new and confusing culture, adults reflecting on their relationships with their parents and children, sojourners traveling back and forth between their own and their host culture and juggling new values as they go, language learners struggling with how to communicate their interesting and complex ideas. There is something here for anyone who has crossed cultures, or wants to understand or explain to others what it's like.

These stories were all written by Asian writers living in the US, members of an International Writers' Club – see the Appendix for a description of how the Club grew and developed in one suburb of Boston under the direction of one of us (Anne Copeland). As such, the stories provide an opportunity to explore differences and similarities among Japanese, Korean and Taiwanese cultures as they intersect with the US American one. But the cultural values revealed in these stories are hardly specific to Asia and the US. Individualism and collectivism, social hierarchy and respect, modesty, high and low context, face and harmony – these are concepts that are important to understand all around the world. And the experience of missing home, seeing one's culture through new eyes, worrying about one's children's values – these are familiar and core to anyone living in a new country.

And so, whether you are a trainer or teacher looking for ways to explain the deep-rooted nature of cultural values, a teacher looking for ways to understand the cultural context within which your students live, or an expatriate looking for insight into your own experience, we hope you will find these stories compelling and useful.

How to Use this Book

This book consists of four main sections:

The Stories: Stories are presented by general theme – Communication, Cultural Adaptation, Customs, and Education. Following each story are several Questions for Reflection, designed to provoke thought among people living in a new culture and all those who are interested in exploring cultural differences in values and habits in their own lives and work. We have highlighted the universality of these stories by phrasing our Questions in ways that are relevant for people from any country.

The Comments: In the second half of the book, we frame each story in intercultural terms, highlighting the themes and dimensions we think the stories illustrate. We suggest you read the stories and answer the Questions first, then turn to the Comments section for further consideration of the intercultural experience of the writers.

The Dimension Descriptions: Because a number of important cultural themes appear repeatedly throughout this collection, we have written a description of them at the end of the collection, rather than repeat this information in each Comment. These Descriptions are very brief summaries of complex, well-researched cultural concepts; we encourage you to supplement this information with further reading.

The Appendix: Here we describe how our Writers' Club was born and the factors we think have led to its success, in case you would like to try to start a Club in your community.

The Indexes: For a list of stories by writers' country of origin, or for a list of stories by the cultural dimension(s) they illustrate, please see the indexes at the end of the book.

Stories

Communication

American Courtesy

The first thing I noticed after I came here, what I heard most was words such as "Hi!", "Excuse me," "I'm sorry" and "Thank you." In the supermarket or any other public place, when someone almost interrupted my way, he/she would say, "I'm sorry." Also it is common to see that one person holds a door open for the next one and the person helped doesn't forget to say, "Thank you." Even if I just made eye contact with someone who had never met me before, we can say to each other with a smile, "Hi!" In addition people usually send a thank you card for a gift on a special day. In the case of children, maybe they will get a goody bag at a birthday party of their friend. Although these words seem to be formal manners, they make a contribution to the enrichment of our lives, I think.

Second, I also hear a lot of words of "compliment and encouragement." Whenever I finished something with difficulty I can hear the words, such as "Perfect!," "Wonderful!," "Good job!," "Excellent!," and "Totally terrific!" Especially, our children hear a lot of the words of praise and encouragement from teachers or other instructors in school and the learning field. I think it is a good fertilizer for the growing tree. Through the experiences in America, I have had a chance again to reflect myself on why I have been so stingy about the expression of emotion and compliments.

Questions for Reflection:

1. The author of this story notes some key differences between the US and her home culture: *"The first thing I noticed after I came here, what I heard most was words such as 'Hi!', 'Excuse me,' 'I'm sorry' and 'Thank you.' In the super-market or any other public place, when someone almost interrupted my way, he/she would say, 'I'm sorry.'* How do these observations compare to your culture?

2. What factors besides nationality influence "friendliness" – City size? Region of country? Similarity of background?

3. Cultures often differ in the interpersonal boundaries that exist – between strangers on an elevator, between parents at a school, between co-workers. Some cultures prefer more privacy, others prefer more openness. It can be hard to have one set of expectations but be living in a country with a different set. Have you ever interacted with someone who has different interpersonal boundaries? What was that experience like? Did you attribute the differences to culture or to personality?

4. In your culture, what are some common approaches for giving feedback? How do these approaches change depending on the context or person (i.e., boss, teacher, mother, friend)? How does this compare to other cultures?

5. The author points out that teachers in the US give a lot of praise and encour-agement to students. What do you think this teaches? How does this compare to other cultures?

Comment: page 123

Apologies

Have you noticed that many Japanese people often mention words of apology? In my case, when I don't understand English, I often say unintentionally, "Sorry, I'm poor at hearing English. I don't understand." I do actually feel bad that they must be patient with my poor English. But I know that I don't say "Sorry" just as a real apology, but also because it is the Japanese way.

When we Japanese really feel sorry, we apologize. But in addition, we use words of apology without thinking deeply, even if we don't really feel sorry. We are not hesitant to apologize to others; rather, it seems to me that words of apology make us relieved not to make friction and to smooth over relationships in our social life in Japan. I think this tendency is one part of our Japanese national character. And we don't have a lawsuit-active society like America. Before I came to America from Japan, I heard that we must not apologize even if we have a car accident.

Another reason why we easily say "Sorry" has to do with the Japanese language. There is one word, "sumimasen," that can mean "thank you," "excuse me," and "sorry" all at the same time. The weight of each of these meanings depends on the situation. For example, if a child gets an unexpected present, we would say, "sumimasen," meaning mostly "thank you." But we also might say, "Sumimasen, can you tell me how to find the library?" Here, we mostly mean, "excuse me." Because this word is ambiguous, it is very convenient. But when I translate this word into English, I just say, "sorry," not its whole, complex meaning.

The other day I found that I lost my daughter's gloves on our way home from the hospital, so I returned to the hospital and asked a receptionist if I might have left her gloves there. She kindly tried to look for them, but my primary doctor had a patient at that time in his room, so she couldn't get in and check it. As soon as I heard her reply,

"Wait a moment," I had said in spite of myself, "Sorry!" I should have said, "Thank you!" We get used to expressing apology for the things we don't need to apologize for.

I like the Japanese way when we communicate between Japanese people. But I think I should pay more attention not to apologize too much in America, because I'm afraid the Japanese's modest way sometimes makes Americans feel strange. Moreover, it is subject to being misunderstood as a lack of self-confidence or misunderstanding.

Questions for Reflection:

1. In your home language, what would you say to a doctor's assistant who tried to find your daughter's gloves?

2. If you speak a second language, have you discovered words that are difficult to translate, for example where you need a phrase or sentence rather than a single word to describe what you mean?

3. Have you ever felt misinterpreted by something you said, because someone did not understand your culture (or subculture)?

4. Under what circumstances do people in your culture apologize? Have you ever expected an apology but not received it? Or, has someone ever surprised you by saying, "I'm sorry" when you did not expect it?

Comment: page 124

Body Distance

One of my favorite American ways is the hugging custom. When I lived in a small rural town in Pennsylvania four years ago, I saw many Americans express their feelings clearly by hugging, kissing or patting shoulders, etc. I was surprised to see this close body contact

done so easily, in a natural way as a salute, not only on emotional occasions but also even when they ran into each other on the street. Of
course, when we are very emotional, we may hug or pat shoulders.
However, we don't usually make body contact with others, even to
our family, in public.

When my American friend hugged me at first, I felt very shy. Here in
Boston, an international city, I'm so interested in observing different
customs. It seems that people from Latin cultures often show more
body contact. When we were invited to my son's friend's birthday
party, who came from Chile, most of the guests and host hugged and
kissed each other warmly. And another time, I can't forget my son's
embarrassed face when his Spanish friend kissed him on his cheek to
see us off from his birthday party.

What I would like Americans and others to understand is that
Japanese are never blank or cool. Although whenever I drop off my
daughter to preschool or pick her up from it, I don't kiss or hug her
dramatically, I love her so deeply, like other mothers. And I would
like them to know that we have body contact with children in other
ways. One is that we often take a good bath time with children in
Japan. Most of our Japanese bathrooms have space where we can
wash off our bodies together. A Japanese-style bathtub is deeper
than American ones and we can bathe in the warmer water up to
our shoulders with our children, playing or singing. (I miss Japanese
bathrooms very much!)

The other is that when we put small children to bed, in their futon
(Japanese style mattress), we often lie down beside them until they
fall asleep. In my case, after reading time, we chat or sing together
quietly for a while in a dark room. My children have been relaxed
with me, listening to my singing lullabies until they go to dream-
land. (And in Japan, babies usually sleep in the same room with
their parents.) Although these Japanese ways have recently changed
to western ways, we have been familiar with the warmth of close
contact for a long time. I believe that these affectionate sharing times

between children and mothers (or fathers) are very meaningful for both of them.

By the way, if you come to Japan and take a crowded train, when somebody's shoulder touches yours unintentionally, even if he or she doesn't say "Excuse me," you shouldn't be offended. It is interesting for me that we don't care about other's body distance on this occasion. I heard that Americans own their personal space, where others are not allowed to come in, and must say "Excuse me" if their body touches another's.

Now personally, I like American hugging. At first, before I hugged somebody, I asked permission, " May I hug you?" But "When in Rome, do as the Romans do." Once I got used to it, I didn't need to ask any more and I find that it is very comfortable. Whenever my friends in America hug me, it makes me so happy and I realize that I'm looking forward to being hugged. Last, please keep in mind that when you do a great favor to a Japanese person, and even if he or she doesn't hug you and just says, "Thank you," smiling at you, the Japanese is absolutely thankful to you.

Questions for Reflection:

1. Under what circumstances do parents and children physically touch each other in your culture? What about children and their grandparents, siblings, and friends?

2. Have you ever come across any different customs that have made you uncomfortable? Have you ever felt that your behavior caused others to feel uncomfortable or to judge you negatively or inaccurately?

3. Have you ever had to adjust to different customs, practices, or values when working or living across cultures, sub-cultures, or organizational settings? If so, how long did that accommodation take you? How would this custom/value fit into your own cultural preferences?

4. Under what circumstances must you apologize for touching someone in your home country? How does that compare to other cultures?

Comment: page 126

The Bow

Korea has often been called "the country of courteous people in the East." Historically, Koreans have considered the rules of etiquette to be the basis of social life. The impolite man is called "sangnom," a careless person who does not know how to behave in a proper Korean manner.

There is a special bowing custom in Korea. It is a greeting custom, like American handshaking, hugs or high-five slaps. We Koreans have two kinds of bows. One is a deep bow that is performed by younger people to elders. It is also performed on New Year's Day and at sacrificial rites. Children usually enjoy the bows on New Year's Day because the elders give money to the bowing children with their good wishes. The other is a little bow. It is done when greeting people and has to be done with a look of modesty and deference about the relationship.

Therefore children have to learn the strict rules of how to bow politely in every situation, because if children act insultingly to elders, people take their parents to task. This is also important work at school in Korea. Children bow at the beginning and end of class. We believe that teachers have a lot of knowledge about education and are quite cultured. We tell our children to keep their heads down while listening attentively to what the teacher says whenever they have made a mistake at school, because Koreans think that teachers are respected the same as parents and will lead our children to a good future. I realize students in the US act quite the opposite in this situation. (Not to look at teachers is considered rude.)

There was an incident about bowing in my child's school. A Korean student was bowing when the teacher was scolding him. However the teacher did not understand his behavior because she mistook the bow for inattention. After that I told my child, "Never bow to an American." But I know that my instruction will have to change some day, because I will have to tell them. "Always bow whenever you meet elders" when we go back to Korea.

Now we are living together in the same world regardless of cultures or customs, so we have to realize that the world would be more harmonious if everyone had a mutual understanding, even if customs seem strange in terms of one's cultural standard.

Questions for Reflection:

1. Is bowing a custom in your culture? If so, who bows to another person, and under what circumstances? To whom have you bowed in your life?

2. Whether or not bowing is common in your culture, how are people of higher status (leaders, teachers, elders) treated differently than others? In your culture, who is treated with the most respect?

3. What is the "correct" way for a child to listen to a teacher who is scolding him/her in your home culture? How does this compare to other cultures you have lived in, visited or learned about?

4. What meaning does eye contact have in your culture? What about in other cultures?

Comment: page 128

English and Japanese Language

When I make a telephone call to tell the school about my daughter's absence, I start by listing her symptoms, and then say she must be absent. In contrast, I think English-speakers might start with the absence, then describe her sickness. We will be struck with great difference if we contrast English with Japanese.

English speakers give main ideas quickly then support the main ideas with lots of details. It looks very rational; however, it is difficult for me to express myself in this way. Our language, Japanese, is indirect and circular. We have to explain many things to support our ideas before we conclude with our main point. However, Japanese are not talkative and we do not like to argue. We were taught, in school and at home, to listen carefully to others rather than express ourselves.

On the one hand, some foreigners criticize the Japanese for not expressing their opinions and for having double standards. However, in the Japanese vertical society, where order is maintained by giving priority to groups rather than individuals, not expressing opinions directly is considered necessary for survival. This tactic of *tatemae* (enunciated principle) is often used in order to solve problems efficiently without hurting anymore; pushing one's opinions too hard tends to be avoided.

On the other hand, I know that direct language speakers do not recognize this Japanese virtue. Specifically, when I talk with Americans, they often ask me what I want to say. The difference in the norms of appropriate speech between English and Japanese can cause miscommunication. Native English speakers who are not familiar with Japanese ways can get frustrated by not being able to get the Japanese speakers' main point as quickly as they expect to. My friend, who speaks English fluently, told me she felt her character was more aggressive when she spoke English.

Although the above examples are applicable both in spoken and in written discourse, speech contains other differences between the two languages. Research findings show that a significantly longer pause is acceptable in Japanese conversation that in English. Japanese speakers are quite comfortable with a long pause, but this can frustrate English speakers. English speakers may find the long pause unacceptable and cut in during the Japanese speaker's turn, hoping to make the conversation flow naturally. However, the interruption by the English speaker can frustrate the Japanese speaker who could not complete her turn. Therefore, when I speak and write in English, I have to change my whole style — how to organize my ideas and my character. However, it is not easy to do. That is why I am too afraid to express myself when I talk with people from other cultures; I feel rude when I say too much and I worry about saying the wrong things.

Questions for Reflection:

1. What communication style is most common in your culture (i.e., direct/ indirect, low/high context, linear/circular)?

2. Have you ever had to communicate with someone with a very different communication style? Was that person from another culture? What was that experience like?

3. Has anyone's communication style ever made you feel uncomfortable, embarrassed, or impatient? Do you think culture had anything to do with it? If so, how?

4. Has your communication style ever made someone else uncomfortable? What was that experience like?

5. Think about the last time you heard someone being rude or aggressive. Is it possible they did not mean to be rude or aggressive, but rather just used a more direct, linear communication style than you expected? Or, think about a time you heard someone being evasive or unclear. Is it possible they were just using an indirect style?

Comment: page 129

Formality and Informality

After I came here, I was embarrassed due to several cultural differences. One of them was the difference in formal meetings. In September, my family and I participated in the welcome party of the school of public health that my husband attends. It was held in the evening. We arrived at the party place on time in order not to miss the introduction of the Dean and other professors of the university.

On arrival, we could see that other students and professors were eating a meal. Maybe the formal event would be after the meal, I thought. It would be good to have a formal event after the meal. I didn't want to wait for the Dean's address while hungry. However, my expectation was not met. After small talk with one another, people left freely. There was no formal event like a Dean's address or professors' introductions.

We had a similar experience at the PTO's meeting of my children's public school. The meeting was only to talk over coffee. The Principal met parents individually with self-introductions. It was not the picture that I imagined.

In my country, a formal meeting is done like this: On time or a little later, the master of ceremony makes an introductory speech with others seated solemnly. Then follows the introduction of professors and administrative staff. It is only after that that participants have a meal.

I can see the good and bad points about this cultural difference. The good points are freedom and versatility. The bad points are lack of solemnity and an inability to get information easily. I felt that active participation was needed to meet other people and get information.

It is impossible to argue the superiority or inferiority of some cultures, I think. They have been formed and modified according to the situations, climates and traditions. They have their own value. However, experiencing other cultures can be a good chance to see good and bad points of our own culture. We can also get the good points of other cultures. I think that we have to try to understand the differences of other cultures and adjust ourselves to them.

Questions for Reflection:

1. In your home culture, would a reception for new students or employees be handled more like what was described in this story, or more like what the author expected? Would people be expected to actively seek information through asking questions and talking to others, or would there be a formal orientation with the same information being given to everyone? What do the different approaches for having a reception reveal about each culture's cultural values?

2. The author points out how informal the event felt compared to her home culture, How do you think the US compares to other cultures on power distance and informality dimensions?

3. What are some ways people show respect (or fail to) in the US? What about in other cultures?

4. Would you feel comfortable chatting with the president of a company (or dean of a university, or the principal of a child's school) on your first day there? Why or why not?

5. Do you agree that "freedom and versatility" are good and "lack of solemnity and inability to get information easily" are bad? Why or why not? Would others from your home country probably agree with her or not? What does this tell you about your own cultural values?

Comment: page 130

Greeting

Recently, I went to Alabama with my husband for his dental school interview. We met a senior professor and shook hands with each other. I felt awkward because handshakes were unusual between a man and a woman in Korea. What was more unusual to me was that he was far older than I. In Korea, I would have had to bow to him.

He was comforting and treated us kindly. He explained to us the facts of dental school. I didn't understand him but I felt warm inside because I realized his kind effort. Soon, I left, saying, "Bye." My husband came to me and said, "Why didn't you shake hands with him when you left? You stood there with your back towards him when he gave you his hand." "Oh, my gosh!" I said. I realized I was very impolite. Handshakes were an unfamiliar way of greeting to me! Although the event lingered long in my memory, I comforted myself since he said that he participated in the Korean War. So I hoped that he would know the Korean culture enough to understand me.

Koreans believe that a handshake with a stiff waist is impolite when they greet older people. Instead, they shake hands with a slight bow. Sometimes Koreans even bow on their knees when visiting elders. They also bow the same way to their parents on New Year's Day and when they are about to leave home for a long period of time.

There is another difference between Koreans and Americans. Most Koreans just greet people they know. When they meet unfamiliar people in an elevator or on a street, they don't greet them. Americans, however, greet anyone that they see with a smile. Therefore, Americans may be surprised at a blunt look from a Korean who is unfamiliar with the American greeting culture.

Since Koreans have lived with Confucian ideas for a long time, they were taught that showing their own feelings before other people is disrespectful. People were also educated that it is disrespectful for a parent to show their feelings of love to their son or daughter in front of their children's grandparents. Koreans have thought that it was part of good manners not to express their good or bad emotions. Therefore, Koreans always find it hard to represent themselves before others.

I am deeply impressed that Americans greet each other delightfully with a smile. When I go back to my country in three years, I will spread the joy I have received here in America onto other unfamiliar people.

Questions for Reflection:

1. What are some differences in how to greet people between your home culture and other cultures? (Kissing on the cheek, bowing, shaking hands, etc.) Have you ever greeted someone in a way that later felt wrong or culturally inappropriate?

2. If you were meeting your spouse's future employer, what personal traits would you want to convey? Would it be more important to look polite and respectful, or confident and open?

3. Do people smile at and speak to strangers on the street in your home country? Do they show their love for their own children in public? What about in front of grandparents? Do these practices vary from other cultures you have been exposed to?

4. Do people from your home country show negative or positive emotions in public? What about at work? In stores? On the bus? Why do you think this is?

Comment: page131

How to React to Compliments

"I saw your son playing soccer very well last Saturday. He is a great, talented soccer player!" If you or your family members get compliments like this, how would you reply? If it is from my American friends, I would say, "Thank you very much! He is crazy for soccer, so he practices a lot." However, if it is from my Japanese friends, I would say, "Oh, no, no. He is not that great. He just had good luck last time."

Generally speaking, I think that this is how we react to compliments. We are expected to be modest, or humble. We think that modesty is a virtue and it is very important to be modest in your daily life. If someone praises us, most of us deny it, even if we think it is true. I am sure that it sounds very strange to many Americans. Even more complicated is that Japanese may think that you are a little arrogant if you don't follow the rule. Lowering yourself in front of others is our basic attitude in almost all situations in Japan. Yes, I know your son is great, but you should deny it, and talk in a modest manner!

How about my children then? I know that here in the US (and many other countries), if someone gives you compliments, you must say, "Thank you!" My children have been in the US for 8 years, so they think in American ways. Because of the difference in culture, I always feel that my children have too much self-confidence. I cannot help telling them to be modest, which my husband and I were told by our parents. Maybe this is why my children don't show their happy feelings in front of their friends.

For example, at the soccer game, my children's teammates show really big pleasure when they win. They scream and hug each other. On the other hand, my sons show only a simple smile and do a high-five.

When my son shot a victory goal at the final soccer tournament, his teammates hugged him and praised him. At the ceremony, his coach and his teammates offered him a champion cup. But my son hesitated to have it and he gave it to the goalie. My son thought the goalie should have the champion cup. Many people didn't understand his behavior. I immediately understood how he took care of his friends. Maybe he accepted something I told him, even though he did not notice that he was doing that. We are always afraid that we just confuse our children when we teach two different cultures, and we understand that it is not easy to cross the border of different cultures. I think that this is a good example of how two different cultures merge.

I don't know which way is better for my children. We should use modesty in several different situations. If we live in the US, you cannot be too modest and you need more self-confidence. If we go back to Japan, we will have to change our attitude. I'm curious how my children learn the American way and Japanese way, and how they digest these two cultures.

Questions for Reflection:

1. What would you say to someone who said to you, "I saw your son playing soccer very well last Saturday. He is a great, talented soccer player!" Would you say "Thank you" or "No no, he just had a lucky day." What are you teaching your child with your reply?

2. Which of these sentences do you agree with more:

   a. A parent's job is to make a child feel special and good about him/herself, so he/she can go on to be a productive adult.

   b. Children naturally feel special and important; a parent's job is to teach them to work well with others.

3. Have you had experiences where you or friends, colleagues or family members have found a way to be "bi-cultural" – that is, to behave one way in one context and another way in a different context?

4. What is good for society about building up children's self-esteem? What is good for society about teaching children to be modest? Probably both are

important. If you had to choose, which one of these would you say is the more important?

5. Have you ever been surprised by someone's modesty (in a situation where you would have expected an enthusiastic display of delight)? Or vice versa — an emotional display when you felt modesty would be more appropriate? What values of theirs and yours are revealed in this situation?

Comment: page 133

I Recommend Your Children Do Sports in America

My sons have tried to do sports in the US. They joined the soccer, swimming, and baseball teams. They like to play baseball best. They enjoy baseball in their third season now. I feel they are always in a comfortable environment. Their coaches always admire their ability with overstatement. If they fail to catch or hit, they say "Good try!" It is a great encouragement to children. Parents also admire their children whether they have a good performance or not. "Wonderful!" "Beautiful!" "Good job, honey!" They speak well with kisses and hugs. How nicely they praise, warmhearted! Children are encouraged by the adults and their teammates.

In Japan, when children join a baseball team, they have to cowboy-up. They have to practice in the early morning and after school for a long time. They are always required to have patience and have guts. They have to build up their body. If they fail to catch or hit, they will be scolded by their coach and parents. "Why can't you catch?" "It is natural that you catch!" I wonder how they feel. Japanese think that children can get into shape by sports. When they do a perfect job, we admire them, saying,"Good job." However, I feel we keep children and parents at a distance.

18

I recommend newcomers do sports here. If they can't speak English at all, they can learn English naturally. They will have a good experience and make friends.

Questions for Reflection:

1. Do you think it is good for children to receive encouraging cheers when they are trying to learn, or is it better to point out what they are doing wrong? Is your answer different for younger vs. older children? What does this reveal about your cultural values?

2. Think of a time when you were learning something for the first time, or doing something that was difficult for you. What kind of feedback was the most helpful to you? Why?

3. What can children learn from playing sports? In your view, is it more important for children to be very skilled at the sport or to really enjoy it even if they are not very good? Why? What does your answer to these questions reveal about your cultural values?

Comment: page 134

I'm Sorry

Have you ever felt that people from Asian countries say, "I'm sorry" too often? If you haven't, please listen to them carefully. There would be no doubt about it. It is true that we say, "Sorry" sometimes when we didn't do anything wrong or make any mistake. At that time, you may be confused. You may think we don't know how to say, "Excuse me."

In fact, the difference between the two, "Sorry" and "Excuse me," is insignificant to us. In America, we often say, "Sorry" instead of "Excuse me." Now you can understand the true meaning of our "Sorry" better than before. We use "Sorry" when we think others will feel uncomfortable because of us. I think it somehow comes out a kind of humiliation, so that we can behave perfectly in this society of different language and culture. We also hope others recognize our attempts to be polite and so understand us better. In some sense, our "Sorry" makes us feel comfortable because it is a kind of prior warning against an impending inconvenience. In other words, our "Sorry" doesn't have such a serious meaning as yours.

On the contrary, Americans say, "Sorry" when they feel it is necessary to say it. When Americans say, "Sorry," they feel really sorry about their behavior and apologize for their mistakes.

Although you may hear Koreans say, "Sorry" in America, in Korea, you don't hear "Sorry" as much as you do in America. We rarely say, "Sorry" to younger people or to people lower in status or power. It is extremely rare for a teacher to say, "I'm sorry" to his student(s). It is also true that a parent almost never says, "Sorry" to his (her) child, nor a governor to his citizens. We try to behave ourselves and become good role models for children, students and citizens. So we need to behave better than we are from time to time. We think we should practice social and moral principles. We don't want to cause others any trouble except when it is inevitable. We try not to make any mistake requiring us to say, "Sorry." We try to do our best to make our behavior perfect. Sometimes we feel it is fatal to say, "Sorry" because we are admitting our faults. So we don't want to say, "Sorry" to persons who are in an equal or inferior level. I think that Buddhism and Confucianism have influenced this aspect of our character.

We're not accustomed to forgiving others, so we can hardly believe that we're forgiven completely. Although we have the occasion to say, "Sorry," we want to deny the fact and avoid saying, "Sorry." We make excuses because we think it is the most shameful thing for us that we need to ask forgiveness from others. In this respect, it seems much easier for Americans to say, "Sorry" than Koreans and other Asians. Our "Sorry" has two sides; one is about an inconvenience and spontaneous action and the other is about asking forgiveness.

Questions for Reflection:

1. Have you heard people say, "I'm sorry when you did not expect it? Have you not heard, "I'm sorry" when you did expect it?

2. Does the author's description of social hierarchies — in which one person is "lower" or "inferior" in status — feel comfortable and familiar to you? Why or why not?

3. Can you think of something you do — like apologize, or smile, or talk about yourself — that may be seen as inappropriate in another cultural context? What cultural rules are you following in each place?

Comment: page 136

Invisibility: Upsetting and Happy Episodes in Daily Life

It happened in a small café in Princeton during spring vacation while my family was visiting the world-famous Princeton University. My husband was in line to get some sandwiches for the girls. He had waited behind two ladies for five minutes then a man came in with his family and just stood by my husband. When it was my husband's turn, the staff asked the other man what he needed first, instead of my husband. He started to order his food, so my husband cut in right away and asked him who came here first? He said, "I'm sorry," and tapped on my husband's shoulder saying, "You go ahead."

After my husband ordered the food, he asked the staff, "You did see me standing here, didn't you?" "No," he said. "I saw nothing." "Short-sighted?" my husband added. (Obviously, he was angry!)

Later when we were walking on the beautiful campus, my husband said, "It's very hard to avoid facing racial prejudice here. It stirs you all the time! No wonder Chinese always stay with Chinese, Americans always stay with Americans. If you don't want to be affected by these trifles, you had better keep away from them…But you can't – It's more and more common to have contact with people of different race, religion, position…" Then my husband looked solemn.

Something similar happened to me when I went to the market. It was my turn and the clerk knew it because we had eye contact, then she skipped me, ignored me like I was an invisible person standing in front of her. Another customer reminded her that it was my turn. I appreciated that. But I can do that – protect my dignity – myself now. And I tell myself that I'll never ever be affected by that. I can't and don't want to keep away from them, and I can keep my mind in purity as a mirror.

Compared with the unpleasant things I mentioned above, I did experience wonderful things in my daily life. Let me tell you one. One day I went into the market and waited to buy some seafood. The clerk was a big woman chatting and laughing with her coworker. When she saw me, she stopped talking and asked me, smiling: "Honey, what can I do for you today?"

Wow! She called me honey!! It's very unusual for a Chinese woman to be called that. I was so happy because I felt like I was accepted completely and immediately. She was definitely a stranger to me, but isn't it amazing that I felt that we were so close!! Later she grinned at me and asked: "Anything else, sweetheart?" Wow-wow!! I gave her my best charming smile that I ever had in my life and said: "Half pound of squid, please."

I knew that she must be in a very good mood that day; I was, too, because of what she called me. For that subtle feeling, I bought lots of seafood that day.

Questions for Reflection:

1. Have you had a time when you felt ignored and discriminated against? What was that experience like? Have you ever seen this happen to others?

2. Being treat as invisible is a passive but powerful way to discriminate. Have you felt ignored or invisible in a way that felt non-accidental?

3. Have you had a time when people were friendlier to you than you expected? Did you like it, or feel uncomfortable?

Comment: page 137

Is This a Really Good Rule?

We don't complain very much in Japan. To complain is not good manners. But I have felt I have had to complain when something wrong happened to us here.

One day at the end of March, the water was shut off in the daytime in our apartment building. We had had one week's notice. It happens several times a year. It was nice for us to be notified a few days before, because I could make a plan to save some water for daytime use or not to stay home. On that day I still did not have water by around 5:30 p.m. It was unusual. After the water comes back on, we always have some trouble. At first we have dirty brown water for a while and also some rusty pieces are stuck in the faucet. So we have to clean them up. On that day, after checking the water for brown pieces, I let my children take a shower. They told me, "The water is too cold. Cold, cold, cold!" My kids had shampoo on their heads and no warm water in the bathtub. It was terrible. So I scooped warm water from the sink with a bowl and gave it to my kids. I believed we would have warm water in the bathtub a little bit later. I took a shower at night and the water was still cold. I felt freezing.

The next morning we asked our neighbor about having warm water in the bath. They said they had no problems. So I went to the superintendent and explained our problem to him. He checked it and he told me it was not a building problem. Our landlord would have to change the faucet, then we would have warm water in the bath. I called our landlord but he was going away for a few days and his wife disregarded our problem. Finally, three days later, our landlord called me and said he would send a handy man to us that night. But the handy man didn't come and he didn't give us a phone call. Then the next day the handy man came but he didn't apologize to us about the day before. The handy man told us that, to fix the faucet and have warm water, the water would have to be shut off. Our house is an apartment. When we shut off the water in the building, all the rooms in a vertical column also have their water shut off We can't shut off water individually. The superintendent told us that we needed to give three days' notice to shut off the water. He told us that weekends didn't count. It was Saturday. So we had to wait until at least the next Wednesday to fix our faucet and to have warm water in the bath. I could not believe the rule, because we couldn't use warm water in the bath for more than one week. It was March, so the cold water was too cold to take a shower. But I could not do anything. And my landlord did not do anything for us. We had to just wait until the Wednesday. The notice said, "Water will be shut off from 1 p.m. to 4 p.m."

On the Wednesday, the plumber didn't come at the appointed time. He arrived later than 3 o'clock. At that time the water was not shut off. So I went to the superintendent to ask about shutting off the water. But it was too late. He just told me, "It is too late to shut off the water. The manager told me. Sorry. I can't do anything." I almost snapped at him. But I felt it was not his fault. I was so disappointed about the plumber and our landlord. The repair date was postponed one week. I was really angry. I could not complain fluently because of my poor English. I was crying because I could not explain my feeling to them. I felt I was at a loss. I called our landlord and left a message: "The plumbers came but they didn't do anything because they came too late. We can't take a shower. I am very angry about it." He didn't call me back that day. And then, the next day he finally came to our house with metal connection parts which connected with a faucet of the sink and a shower hose. He finally apologized to us. But my feeling was not good. He put the shower hose to the faucet of the sink. It was better because we could take a shower with warm water from the faucet of the sink. But at the same time, it was inconvenient because we could not use the sink or faucet as usual. Whenever my kids used the faucet I had to go and help them. Finally, after 15 days we had warm water in the bath tub. At that time all of our family had colds because the shower time was too cold for us.

We couldn't take a shower because we didn't have warm water in the bath. I think it was an emergency. But the building rules were so strict and ridiculous. I think rules should have more flexibility, because rules are for people and they should make people comfortable.

Questions for Reflection:

1. Would this situation have happened in your home country? What would you have done there, if it happened to you? Can you guess what you would have done in the author's situation?

2. Are there rules to protect tenants in your home country? What happens if the landlord breaks those rules?

3. Have you ever had the experience of not being able to speak a second language well enough to accurately express the frustration (or other strong emotion) that you felt? What was that experience like?

Comment: page 138

Meaning of "Yes" or "No" to Answer Negative Questions

There are so many people and tribes using different languages in the world. It is not easy in general to understand foreigners' communications because of this language barrier. In spite of the difficulty to learn foreign languages, "Yes" and "No" could be the easiest words for learning and using a new language, since the meaning of the two words seems clear in all languages. However, "Yes" and "No" also cause confusion in communication, especially in the case of negative questions.

For example, here is a conversation between two people who love each other.

> *Man*: Do you want to marry me?
> *Woman*: Yes, I do.
> *Man*: I am happy to ask you one more time. Don't you want to marry me?
> *Woman*: No, I do.
> *Man*: What? Don't you want to marry me?
> *Woman*: No, I really want to marry you.
> *Man*: Do you mean yes or no?
> *Woman*: No matter whether I say yes or no, it is true that I want to marry you.

If an American woman answers like the transcript, she must be insane because of the unexpected proposal for marriage from her lover. However, if the woman is a Korean, the answers are fine, due to a unique usage and meaning of "Yes" and "No" in Korean. To answer positive questions, the two words are used in Korean the same as in English. But, for negative questions, "Yes" and "No" mean totally different things in Korean compared to English.

This is in contrast to the usage of "Yes" and "No" in English, which is always identical to the listener's opinion – the English listener answers in terms of the content of the question – "Yes, I want to marry you" or "No, I don't want to marry you" – not the form of the question.

In the Korean language, an answer needs to show the listener's assessment of whether the questioner's thought is right or wrong, and then describes what the listener is willing to do. Therefore, "Yes" means the listener agrees with the questioner's thought – "Yes [you are right], I don't want to marry you" and "No" always comes up with an idea that must be opposite to questioner's expectation – "No [you are wrong], I don't want to not marry you." Because "Yes" and "No" in Korean are differently used in the answers for negative questions compared with English, many Koreans are frequently hesitant and confused about how to answer when someone asks a negative question. Isn't it funny and interesting? "Yes, it is" or "Yes, it is not."

Questions for Reflection:

1. How do you answer negative questions in your home language? Say you want to go to a store. If someone says to you, "Don't you want to go to the store?" would you say "Yes" or "No?"

2. Under what circumstances do you use negative questions in your home language? Do they usually imply that the listener will agree with you ("Don't you think it's cold in here?" "Aren't you hungry?" "Isn't this a great TV show?")

3. Can you think of any cultural values that are reflected in your language?

Comment: page 139

Mosquitoes

I came to America full of expectation. When I visited the school, I was very happy because of a lot of kind teachers, and clear, quiet and convenient buildings. But my children didn't have much time to become friendly with American classmates, because summer vacation began as soon as they started to go to the school. So I enrolled them in a summer sleepover camp.

There were lakes and a forest. The place was good. But I worried there were too many mosquitoes. I really wanted mosquitoes not to bite my son, so I talked to the nurse. She said to me, "Don't worry. No mosquitoes will bite your son and if something is wrong with your son, I'll just call you back." Therefore, my husband and I returned to my house with relieved minds. We visited the camp three times to try to meet my son. At last, when I met my son, we were really, really surprised at my son's face because mosquitoes bit his whole body from face to feet. Mosquitoes bit my son while he slept because there was a hole in the cabin next to his bed.

But nobody took care of my son. The nurse didn't call me and when we asked her about this, she said that there was no problem. The chief of the camp also said, "No problem." I don't understand. We came back home with my son; after that we took care of him and helped him to relax. We gave him an ice massage and gave him antihistamine and antibiotics for his bites. The next day when we visited the camp, we asked for a refund. The chief said, "You should visit the Y next Monday." We visited the responsible person at the Y even though she never tried to see my son. "If you want a refund, you should submit a document of a pediatric diagnosis."

Therefore, we asked for the refund, because my husband is a cardiologist and a professor for sixteen years in Korea. So, we thought my husband's opinion would be accepted and then they would refund it. However, they refused to refund it. I really can't understand why

the word of an expert couldn't be accepted. If this same situation occurred in Korea, the chief would visit us directly and apologize about
this bad incident. I can hardly understand this part of American
culture.

Questions for Reflection:

1. What surprised you about this story? If you had been at the author's side during this episode, what might you have said to her at each step?

2. If you had been the camp nurse, what might you have done differently to avoid
this outcome? What if you had been the head of the Y?

3. If this situation happened in your home country, would the father's letter be
sufficient to get a refund? Why or why not?

4. Why wasn't the author's husband's letter sufficient to obtain a refund in this
particular cultural context? What values are revealed in her expectation that
the letter would work, and in the US stance that it would not?

5. In Korea, the author tells us, the Y "chief" would have visited the family and
apologized. What cultural differences are revealed here?

6. If you had moved to a new country, put your child in a program recommended
by neighbors, then found out that he/she had not received the medical care
you considered basic, and then felt you had gotten a run-around from the
authorities, what would you do? (Try to answer this question even if you do
not think it is an adequate characterization of what happened here.)

7. Have you had to get medical care for yourself or a family member or had to
complain about a service, product or experience while outside of your home
country? What role did language, culture or anxiety play in your experience?

Comment: page 140

My Struggle with Discipline and Praise

When coming to the United States, I was so surprised at several differences between the United States and Japan as to how children are treated by adults. For example, praise and discipline are very different in public settings, schools and extracurricular classes.

Four years ago, when I entered a rest room at the Mall, I saw a mother praising her daughter who was three years old, saying "Good job", "Wonderful", "Excellent!" while washing and drying her hands. Then I felt a little bit embarrassed seeing it. I was unaccustomed to it. In Japan, a mother might say to her child "Wash more neatly " and "Dry your hands completely," etc.

I have some experiences in the United States with parent-teacher conferences at my sons' school. The teachers told me many good things about my kids. I could not remember the bad things easily. In Japan, teachers tell parents some faults and that kids ought to change their attitude and behavior.

My oldest son is taking Kendo classes once a week. Kendo is a traditional Japanese martial art similar to fencing. It uses strong discipline to learn concentration, perseverance and respect. Recently, at Kendo class, my son was crying after class had already finished. I asked him why he was crying. He said the teacher was so strict to him and disciplined him publicly. I thought he felt depressed because he has not had many experiences like that. When his dad and I were children, teachers were often so strict like this. We understood what they wanted to say or make us do. Then we could respond to their requirements. We believe that is one of the ways kids' minds will become stronger. We also think it is important to encourage and praise them after strict teaching and discipline.

On the other hand, he is on a baseball team in our town. His team's coaches are tremendously eager and are always encouraging the players. Even when my son strikes out swinging, they say, "Beautiful swing!" or "Good eyes." I think he does not have self- reproach and he feels positive because of this gentle method.

I am always confused how to use a good mix of discipline and praise. That situation is completely different from my childhood. Sometimes my kids disagree with me or do not understand what I want to explain about thinking and behavior. They have already been in the United States for four years, so my Japanese style is a little uncomfortable for them. We have to go back to Japan next year, so I worry about whether they can become accustomed to Japanese life or not. I hope they will have a smooth transition from life in the United States to life in Japan and be able to fuse both cultures and adjust well to real life in the world.

Questions for Reflection:

1. In your home country, do parents and teachers tend to offer more praise to children or more instructions on how to improve? What do you see as the advantages and disadvantages of each approach? What cultural value or message does each approach promote?

2. What do you think is the best thing for parents to do if they want their children to succeed in a new culture while also benefiting from their own values?

3. Under what circumstances (if any), do you think is it better to reward a child's effort, even if his/her outcome is not perfect? Under what circumstances is it better to insist on a better outcome?

4. Do you think it is best for children to be raised just like you were?

Comment: page 142

North is Always on Top of the Map

I have a very bad sense of direction. However, I recently noticed a cross-cultural issue contributing to it.

I had a chance to go sightseeing in Spain with my American colleague. At a train station, I watched how my colleague read the map and noticed one thing. First he looked for the name of the station where we were, and then the name of the previous station. This was to see which direction the train was going on the map. To my great surprise, it was going in the opposite direction from what I believed. Standing on the station we saw trains coming from the right, but the map looked as if the same train would come from the left! I had to turn this map upside down in my head in order to make more sense - right is right and left is left. I wondered why they did such a complicated thing. Isn't it more reasonable to draw a map that is parallel to the actual direction of the train?

North is always on top of the map in the US. My son is learning how to use a compass, read maps, and give directions at his school in the US. I checked with his teacher, and she confirmed that maps in the US always show North at the top.

North is usually on top of the map in Japan, but it is not always true. In Japan, in atlases and driving maps, north is, of course, on top. But it is not always true for a guide board in a town, a map at the train station, and especially handwritten maps for inviting people to your home. Sometimes a compass is drawn on such a map to show which direction is North, but not always. Why? That is because we do not use South or North, East or West in giving directions.

There is an interesting essay written by an American professor living in Japan for more than 20 years. When he had a party at his home, he explained the directions to one of his Japanese friends. He said, "There is a big park southeast of the train station. Take the street on

the west of the park toward the south, then you will find my apartment." Another Japanese friend who was listening to him warned
him that his friend would never get to his apartment with that explanation. She said she would give the same direction like this: "At the
gate of the station, turn right. There is a flower shop. Turn right at
the corner of the flower shop. You will see an ice cream shop on your
right. Pass that ice cream shop and go straight for about 100 meters.
There is a house with rose garden. My apartment is next to it."

This explicitly shows the difference between Japan and the USA (or
Western society) in the way to give directions. As the professor ex-
claimed, we Japanese use tiny landmarks to find our direction, rather
than using universal and absolute measures of North, South, East and
West. We set a tiny landmark and give directions to the right or left
from that landmark. We do not even think of whether the direction
is South or North. In that sense, it is not surprising that a map could
easily be written with South on top.

I do not know which way is superior. But I am sure that in Japan,
some travelers from different parts of the world will look at a map at
the station and go in the opposite direction!

Questions for Reflection:

1. Would you prefer to have directions to a party given in terms of North, South,
   East and West, or in terms of landmarks? Which is more common in your
   home country?

2. Would you consider your culture to be more "high context" or "low context"?

3. What are some other examples of how these cultural dimensions play out in
   your culture or other cultures?

Comment: page 143

The Reason Why We Are Silent

In Japan, the roots of our society are feudalistic. So, for a business-man, it is still very hard and dangerous to raise an objection to his boss. After an argument, he might be relegated to an inferior position. In schools, when students are scolded by their teachers, they had better not defend themselves, or they might be scolded harder.

In my own childhood, when my mother scolded me, sometimes I defended myself and got an even longer scolding. So I used to keep silent and at last said, "Sorry." It was the best way to make it short-est, even if my mother said "Why are you keeping silent? Tell me what you are thinking." I think some Japanese children have the same experience, though most of them and their mothers have more democratic relationships and the children feel free to talk to their mothers.

Generally, Japanese hesitate to insist on their opinion or defend themselves (especially to elder people), and easily say "Sorry," so as not to make the situation worse. In the US, this is a problem. Actu-ally, I have heard that one Japanese boy was scolded by his teachers and was expected to defend himself, but he did not. Therefore he was rebuked for it. In the case of newcomer children, when they are scolded by their teachers, three factors encourage them to be silent: first, the Japanese hesitation; second, their trouble speaking English; and third, their complicated emotions from having been frustrated at not having the English skill to be able to say what they mean. And sometimes they say "Sorry," just to be liberated early without thinking.

Please understand that we Japanese also have our own opinions but we are always afraid about whether they will be accepted or not. It's our habit. Because in our society, we think much of harmonious personal relations, unusual opinions (and behavior and even dress) are difficult to accept. And problems speaking English spur us on to being silent.

Questions for Reflection:

1. Have you noticed a difference between the US and other cultures in people's comfort with silence? Under what circumstances does silence become uncomfortable for you? How does that compare to other cultures?

2. What is the right thing for children to do when being scolded by a teacher in your home country? Why?

3. Do you know people you think are too deferential – that is, they seem to say "Sorry" too much or not defend themselves even when they know they are right? Does this story lead you to think differently about them?

4. Do you know people you think are too aggressive – that is, they argue when they should apologize? Does this story lead you to think differently about them?

Comment: page 144

Talk to Strangers

When I get with someone in an elevator, Americans always talk to me and our children, such as, "It's a beautiful day" and, "How was school?" And sometimes the other people who happen to be there break in as if it were his/her own conversation. Of course they are strangers I've never met before. Even when I pass someone on the road and our eyes meet, the person says, "Hi!"

In such a case, we rarely talk to strangers in Japan. If we have known each other by sight, we may greet with a nod. Even more, we rarely break in on other people's conversations. To break in on another person's conversation is considered rude for us. If we can hear their conversation, we may act deaf as if we didn't know. Sometimes silence is considered a virtue for us. In fact I had never talked with my neighbor who had been living next door, in Japan. Japanese love to stand in line to eat Ramen, but even if we are standing in line for more than one hour, we don't talk to the people around us.

I have been feeling nervous about getting on an elevator with some-
one since I started living in the US, as I didn't know how to act there.
When I am spoken to by a cashier at a supermarket ("How are you?"),
I may say, "Fine," even if I am not in good shape.

Though Americans talk to strangers very easily, it is interesting for
me that they don't ask any personal questions, even to their acquaintances, such as "How old are you?" or "Do you have a child?" and so
on. We often ask that kind of question even when we meet someone
for the first time. The Japanese language has honorific expressions
and we use them to pay our respect to our senior and elders. So we
sometimes need to know if the person is older than us or not.

Now more than one year has passed since I moved to the US. Recently I have started being comfortable talking with strangers anywhere. The other day I talked to an old lady next door, who was
putting on a beautiful pink hat. I told her naturally what a beautiful
hat she was putting on, and she told me about it, saying she had had
the hat for 35 years. It looked especially beautiful and heartwarming
for me. If I had not talked to her about it, I would have had no way of
finding out her story.

When I go back to Japan, the other way, I will miss strangers talking
to me. It may not be easy to change our cultures, however I will try
to talk to strangers who come from other countries and even to Japanese just as the Americans did.

Questions for Reflection:

1. Have you ever been surprised by a stranger speaking to you? Whether yes or
   no, what does this tell you about your cultural expectations?

2. In the US, people may chat casually with each other to fill in a silence that
   feels uncomfortable to them. How is this similar or different to other cultures?

3. In your home language, do you use a different vocabulary to speak with people older than you? How much older do they have to be to warrant this different vocabulary? What does this practice demonstrate about cultural values?

4. Think of a time you have adopted the value or behavior of a new culture. What factors led to the change? How long had you been exposed to the new culture before the change occurred? Have you had the chance to return to your home country — and if so, how does this new value fit there?

Comment: page 145

Too Much Caring About Others' Thinking

I was the only left-handed child in my family. When my parents realized it, they tried to fix my lefty. I had to use my pencil or chopsticks with my right hand and it was very difficult and stressful for me. When I entered elementary school, I gradually used my left hand and at last my parents gave up. But they still insisted that I use my right hand at meals, because it was bad manners, and they thought if I used my left hand, I might disturb people sitting to my left side. They said, "Everybody is looking at you, so please behave well." Of course, they were strict about bad things (for example, telling a lie or teasing somebody), too; they also very much cared about other people's response to these things.

Nowadays, young Japanese people (maybe including me) care about other people's feelings less than people my parents' age. But we still worry about others' thinking. I think Japanese parenting and discipline are always related to others' thinking. Sometimes, there is too much caring about others. Is it because Japan is an island or Japanese are a homogeneous race?

Questions for Reflection:

1. Are left-handed children in your home culture urged/forced to be right-handed? Why or why not?

2. What are some of the ways parents in your home culture care about what others are thinking? That is, are there kinds of child behavior they try to change because of what other people will think? What are some of the ways parents in your home culture teach children to be respectful of others — for example, of others' comfort, privacy, or freedom? In these cases, is the parent's emphasis on what others will think or on what will be good for the child or the other people in the culture?

3. Why might island or homogeneous cultures be more likely to teach children to be concerned with what others are thinking? Do you think this is true? Why or why not?

4. Are there things you do (or don't do) when others might see you, but not when you are alone? How would you categorize these things? What does it teach you about your values that these should/may be kept private?

Comment: page 147

Cultural Adaptation

Call Me Stupid,
But Whose Responsibility is Fraud?

In general, Japanese people like the United States and respect its people very much. Many Japanese think the United States is a country that symbolizes liberty, power and prosperity. So, when our family moved to California, I felt like I was on the top of the world. People were very kind and helpful, and wherever I went, places were so spacious and wheel chair-friendly (that means stroller-friendly; my daughter was one year old at that time) and there was a variety of high quality adult education classes!! Everything looked great!

That euphoria ended when I received a telephone call one day. Looking back, the telephone bell sounded like, "Welcome to the dark side of the United States!" A man said, "May I speak to Mrs. Yamazaki?" (He knew my family name.) When I said, "Speaking." He said, "This is a credit card security company. This is a card emergency. I was asked by your husband to contact you about your card." His words threw me into a panic. "Oh, no. Oh, no. What should I do?" Then he said, "Calm down. It's OK. We can help you, but in order to facilitate our service, may I record our conversation?" I said, "Yes." Then he said, "Is your credit card number, xxxxxx?" Of course I didn't memorize my credit card number. So I said, "Wait, wait. Let me check the number. No, it's xxxxxx." I blurted out my number. Then he said, "We are going to charge you $650 for the protection against future damage. Say 'Yes' now— -." "Wait a minute." I finally noticed something was wrong. I hung up the phone and caught my husband at his lab. I asked him if he had asked a credit card security company to contact me. He said, "I have no idea what you are talking about. Call the credit card company in Japan immediately and ask them to stop the usage of your card!" I did. Thank goodness, no harm was done.

I delivered my son at a university hospital. When I left the hospital, they gave me a lot of direct-mail offers. Among them was a catalog of children's picture books. I ordered some books by mail. I received those books several days later. I noticed for the first time that the shipping and handling fee was ridiculously expensive. What was worse, they started continuously sending me many books I had never ordered. Flabbergasted, I called the company and asked them what I should do. They told me to simply send them back, which I promptly did. Then I received a blackmailing letter, saying that I purchased the reasonable books when I became a member of that company. If I wanted to quit my membership, I would have to buy two children's books at $30. (The actual value of those books was about $10 dollars at most.) At that time, I learned from TV that it took prosecutors more than ten years to indict a company that sold their products to their customers by saying, "Congratulations! You've won a lottery, but in order to get the money, you have to buy theses dolls at $20 first."

Of course, the same kinds of problems do exist in Japan, too, but to this extent? No way! In the US, I often encounter expressions like "She was at the wrong place at the wrong time" when somebody was raped or killed. When somebody had her purse stolen, "She should have been more careful." When somebody got conned, "How could she be so stupid?" So, tell me please. In this country, is it a victim's fault, not the criminal's, if you get into some trouble?

Questions for Reflection:

1. Have you ever witnessed any kind of fraud? Whom did you blame and why? What does this reveal about your own cultural beliefs?

2. Think of three unfortunate things that have happened to you or someone you know recently — they do not have to be major events (for example, you left your credit card in a restaurant, or you got sick and missed your son's school play, or a taxi driver charged more than you think was fair). Do you think about whether someone was to "blame" in each instance, and if so, who? What kinds of things deserve "blame" or "credit," as opposed to being just bad luck? Where there is fault, do you tend to blame the criminal or the victim or both?

3. Do you consider yourself, or most people in your culture, to have high effort optimism or low effort optimism? What are some other examples of how this cultural dimension plays out in day-to-day life?

Comment: page 148

Deciding Whether to Move to a Foreign Country

I was introduced by email to a man by my friend. He will go abroad to the USA one year from now and will be staying for two years. He has a wife and three children and he is wondering whether he should move with his family or not. He wanted to hear from me about moving to the USA, especially about the behavior of our children at that time because we came here all together from the first.

His children will be an 11-year-old girl, 7-year-old boy and 5-year-old boy at the time of their move, one year from now. According to his e-mail, his two sons are excited about moving to the USA, but his daughter refuses to do it because she simply can not bear to leave her friends in Japan. She once transferred to another school in her first grade in Japan because of her father's job and she had difficulty making new friends in her new school. That experience had a considerable impact on her.

His wife is an elementary school teacher and she also was having difficulty thinking of leaving her career behind. So he was thinking about moving here with his two sons and leaving his wife and daughter in Japan.

Our children were 5 years old, 3 years old and 1 year old at the time we moved. They were too young to have any close friendships in Japan, so they showed little resistance to the change in their surroundings. And I didn't worry about whether we should take our children or not. But his story made me think about how the changes in our environment affected our children. I was also a working mother in Japan, but I didn't hesitate to resign my job. Moving to a foreign country with our whole family and setting up our new life seemed very exciting and valuable to me.

In terms of the benefits of living abroad for children, people often mention the acquisition of their second language. I think it is more wonderful especially for Japanese children to go out of our so-called "almost mono-racial society" and find out that there are many kinds of people who have varied skin colors, varied hair colors and varied mother languages, in other words, to experience naturally that they are just one part of the diversity in the world.

And it might be good for them to have had some bitter experiences they might not have had if they were living in Japan. For instance, my children couldn't join their new friends at first in their child care setting, because they didn't speak English at all. They had difficulty telling their feelings and requests to their teachers in English. Such experiences themselves will be food for their mind and heart and help them to consider others. It is natural for parents to hope their children live without getting hurt as far as possible. But I think children will expand the range of their ideas and acquire strong minds by having bitter experiences little by little in their childhood. Of course, children are getting to live positively because they have a lot of happy experiences which make up for their bitter experiences.

I hope all of their experiences here will provide a powerful underpinning for my children when they become "newcomers "again after their return to Japan in the future.

Questions for Reflection:

1. How would you advise the man who consulted the author about whether to move his family to the US? Should the family do as the father proposed and split (males here, females there) for two years? How resilient are children?

2. In your home country, could a woman stop working as an elementary school teacher for several years, then return to it? How, if at all, does this vary across the cultures you are familiar with? Could a mother like the one in this story re-enter the teaching professional upon return in your country?

3. What would children learn from living in another country that they would/could not learn from staying in their home community?

4. How does the US differ from other countries in how multi-cultural or multi-racial it is? What would children learn from living in a multi-cultural society that they would/could not learn from living in a mono-cultural one?

5. Have you had a "bitter" or difficult intercultural experience that you now see as having taught you a valuable lesson? Do you think it's a good idea to protect children from bitter experiences? Why?

6. What circumstances would keep you from moving to another country? What circumstances would be compelling enough to lead you to accept such an opportunity? Why?

Comment: page 149

Going Home Again

One year ago, when my husband told me that he was admitted to Harvard and he wanted us to go with him, I was really shocked. That meant I should leave my family, friends and country and enter into another unfamiliar environment. It was a big challenge to me. I felt so nervous, excited, hesitant and sometimes reluctant. These complicated feelings disturbed me until I determined to go.

America is the strongest country in the world. I have been eager to visit there since I was young. Now my dream had come true. Most of my friends were so envious. They always said, "How wonderful! You are so lucky. I bet you will not come back." "Yes, I will want to come back. I love my country and love you all. Trust me. I will be back," I answered in a strong tone. Although America is like a magnet, and magnetizes so many immigrants from all over the world, I told myself that I wouldn't be one of them.

It has been really tough work to adjust myself to a new culture. My English is not good. I could neither speak nor understand very well. If someone spoke to me more than three sentences, I would be lost. It made me upset, embarrassed and uncomfortable.

Further, the subway train is so slow, the pavement is unsmooth, the shopping center is so boring, and American food is disgusting. I seldom eat out, because everything is so expensive. I felt disappointed and started to hate the city, the country, the people, the apartment and everything else.

Two months later, one day I woke up, I saw the sun shine through the window into my home. The foliage was vivid and colorful outside. And I thought of my three children educated in the elementary school without paying. The teachers are kind. The teaching is so creative. My kids enjoy their school very much. There are so many playgrounds for children to play outside. I appreciated that America gives us so much. I told my children to keep in mind that they should give back to America in the future. We have become accustomed to live here day by day.

Last month, I had some important things to deal with so I traveled back to Taiwan. During those two weeks, an unreasonable fear came up in my mind and I felt disorientated. Taipei is so crowded, humid, noisy and air-polluted. I couldn't drive because of terrible traffic jams. It was a big stress to me to walk across the street. I couldn't imagine this familiar environment to be the place I've lived in for decades and just left seven months ago. The feelings impacted me in the same way as I just came to America. I thought it is reverse culture shock.

Questions for Reflection:

1. The author shared her struggles with culture shock, and then explained how she entered a phase of acceptance and adjustment to her host culture. What struggles have you faced (or do you anticipate facing) in dealing with culture shock?

2. Have you ever had the experience of going back home to your home culture after having lived abroad (or living in another part of the country)? What was that experience like?

3. Have you ever experienced culture shock? What did it feel like?

4. What are the different phases of culture shock described in this story?

Comment: page 150

Hurry Up

I think everything has two sides. One side is positive and the other, negative. I am going to tell you about the American and Korean concepts of time, based on my experience. As you know, the United States is geographically huge but Korea is small and therefore crowded.

On settling here, I needed to get an American driver's license. One day, I went to the Registry of Motor Vehicles with my husband to take the exam. There were lots of people who were waiting for document processing. I waited in the line for a long time. But the staff who were working in the RMV never hurried up serving people. They were drinking Coke or coffee, eating, and talking with their neighbors about things unrelated to their jobs. I supposed if they considered the many people who were having to wait for a long time, they could have worked more effectively or faster.

"Time is gold." As I mentioned before, my country is not only small but we have a shortage of natural materials. Seventy percent of my country is mountains. We have had to create value from nothing. That means we have had to make more effort than people in other countries and to save time through good organization. Wherever we go, we want to spend the exact time needed there. Whatever we do, we want to do it very effectively, saving time, even if it is hard to do. Almost all Koreans, including me, want to save time in everything, even eating. It may look like we are always hurrying. In fact, we think we are able to save the time effectively only when we hurry up.

There is another difference between Korea and the US. In Korea, we usually don't need to make an appointment to do something, even at a hospital. Everybody is treated by "first come first served." This also contributes to a "hurry up" sense.

When I came here, I was not patient in waiting, but now I am adapting and am more patient, waiting in line and making appointments. I may organize the time wisely. In summary, now I can say time can be used wisely and effectively and saved, even if we don't hurry up. On the other hand, American staff need to use their time more effectively. Probably they could do something more for people in this way.

Questions for Reflection:

1. How does the pace of service at government offices in the US compare with your home country?

2. In general, how does the pace of work and living in the US compare with your home country? Have you noticed a change in your own pace?

3. How has the geography of your home country influenced its values or customs?

Comment: page 152

Making Friends

For me, making friends with Americans is the same as making friends in Japan. Of course, at first, I hesitate to use my poor English, but if we found the same interests or same feeling that we would like to know each other, the process is the same.

Sometimes, I am surprised that our common sense is not shared by my American friends. For example, when Japanese visit a friend's house, even if we just pick up the child from a play date, we usually bring something. Furthermore, we might say, "This is nothing wonderful, but I hope you like it." (Of course, we just think modesty is good, and we never prepare a worthless gift!) But here, I learned we don't need to send a snack for a play date and it is not rude.

I also learned Americans don't understand too much modesty. When I pick up my son from his friend's house, many people ask me to tour their house. I hesitate to enter the house and wait at the hallway or gate. But I heard they couldn't understand why I hesitate so much and explained it was a normal manner. In Japan, we will wait at the hallway or gate, if we are not invited. We think this is etiquette. But if we respect each other, our misunderstanding is easily removed and we can find a new way of thinking. It is very exciting to know a different world.

I think generally, Americans have such different backgrounds (race or culture) that they accept foreigners or different thinking easily. In my view, the Japanese are a single race and prefer the same thinking, so it takes a long time to accept foreigners or different thinking. (My name is uncommon in Japan. Especially before I changed my name to the Japanese style, it was very hard for me to make friends in Japan.) Because my thinking is more Japanese, still now and because of my careful personality, I don't show my privacy or weakness at first.

But whether my friend is American or Japanese, I believe I will be able to talk about everything later after we make a good friendship.

Questions for Reflection:

1. Do you have any friends from a different culture than your own? What about acquaintances? Have you noticed any differences in expectations or customs between you and those you know from other cultures?

2. Think of a time when you have been disappointed in or surprised by something a potential friend from another culture did. What were you expecting, and what happened instead? What does this tell you about your expectations and his/hers?

3. Can you think of any example when your idea of "common sense" was not shared by another person? Can you identify any cultural values or expectations that informed your or the other person's idea of "common sense?"

On the Street

"How strange and frightening it is!"

At first, I was afraid of the New World when I arrived at Logan Airport, Boston, in December. The weather was very cold and it was snowing heavily. The houses, buildings, signs, cars, and people on the street were different from Seoul, Korea. There was nobody I knew. And there were so many things that I didn't know. I didn't know how to read a map, how to speak in English, where to go shopping, whom to meet or how to use an ATM. My English was too poor to speak and understand everything of the New World. I worried about every-thing.

In Korea, I was happy with my everyday routine and did not like to try new things. I thought, "To live in America, I need to be brave and positive." So I made up my mind to be active and strong. I told myself not to act shy.

Boston is one of the oldest cities in America. The streets are too nar-row and it is difficult to drive a car. Many pedestrians in crosswalks don't follow the traffic rules. They cross the street anywhere, but I expected them to follow the traffic lights.

Seoul, Korea is one of the biggest cities in the world. There are many people and cars on the street. Many cars rush so fast, the drivers don't think about the people crossing the street. They think they are more important than pedestrians. Their way of thinking is very dan-gerous and selfish.

I thought the subway in Boston was very old and unclean. However, the street signs were very clear. It was not difficult for me to find roads, because there were many signs. "Stop" signs were very annoying for me, because in Seoul, there aren't many stop signs. People just look both ways and continue driving. But I admit that we need signs now.

Another thing was the way drivers react when an ambulance is roaring down the street. It's known that drivers must move aside to the right when one of these vehicles is coming up behind them. However, in Korea drivers are less likely to yield in the same situation. The way Koreans deal with this situation should make us feel ashamed.

I was scared and clueless when I stepped foot in America. How far I have come! I'm not afraid anymore. I take my chances and I even have the guts to drive through strange and unfamiliar places without being that nervous.

I hope that while I'm here, I'll be able to gain more experiences and confidence. I will try to help Americans to know about Korean culture.

Questions for Reflection:

1. Describe a driving custom that you have observed in one location (country, city, region) but not another. Have you ever adopted a new driving custom after living where it is common?

2. Think of a time when you went through a transition (i.e. going from high school to college, moving to another culture, or changing jobs).What personal characteristics were most important to you as you went through that transition? How, if at all, were you different after that experience?

3. Describe one thing that seemed difficult when you first went through that transition, but that then seemed easier. Why did it become easier?

Comment: page154

Parent-Child Relationships in the USA

I think most American children do not want to look up to their parents as a model. In fact, parents try to do their best to keep up with their children. It shows us a value held by Americans: "newness" has more value than "following tradition." It is a typical American value, rooted in their pioneer history.

The USA is a country of immigrants. The first generation to immigrate from their own country could often not acquire American culture such as its language, food, or life style, even though they had made every effort to blend in with the country. They made restricted communities: China town, Little Tokyo, Polish town, or Puerto Rican town. Then they laid their hopes on and entrusted their dreams to the second generation to be more American.

First generation immigrants can seldom become good models for their children in the USA. If the second generation completely modeled the first generation, the second generation could not become as fully American as they can. Indeed, the second generation has often denied the first generation, so they can fit into America.

Sometimes children even have to be teachers for their parents. Children learn correct English pronunciation, American life style, American values, and so on. Parents learn those things from their children.

My daughter wants to take the initiative among us recently. She often points out our incorrect English pronunciation or does not share our opinion about our customs. She might try to overcome us and be an American by naturalization. I sometimes feel sad about it because I am losing my authority over my daughter. Now she is losing her Japanese because I eagerly want her to be an American. In addition, we have difficulty communicating with each other little by little. Since her vocabulary increases explosively with her growth, I have been looking up words in a dictionary when I speak to her. I am afraid that someday we will not be able to have satisfactory communication or a good relationship. Recently, I really feel uneasy about the delicacy and difficulty of relationships between the first and second generations of immigrants.

Questions for Reflection:

1. What is a parent's job — to teach the wisdom of his/her own values, or to teach the child to think for him/herself?

2. Do you agree that "most American children do not want to look up to their parents as a model. In fact, parents try to do their best to keep up with their children?" In general, do you think it is good for society for children to try out new things or for them to adopt their parents' tried-and-true ways?

3. The author highlights a situation in which her children's cultural future is likely to be very different from her own, and wonders how (and whether) she can be a model for them. Do you think children can turn to adults as models even if the adults are quite different from them?

4. Think of three values that are very important to you. Were those values shared by your parents? Are there any values that you feel strongly about passing on (or not passing on) to your own children?

Comment: page 155

The Picture of Homeland

Our family recently went back to Taiwan for three weeks. It was a great experience to explore the culture that I was familiar with again. The picture of my homeland that I keep in my mind has changed again and again since I came here two years ago. Initially, I missed my family, friends, the food, the convenience and the easy life. But as time went by, the feeling of missing home faded. I got used to the food, the driving, and the not-so-easy but peaceful life here. Friends and activities filled my life and made it colorful. I love that my family could be together and develop a solid relationship here. Day by day, I didn't think too much about my country.

Of course, deep in my heart, the homeland picture was always there and called me back. After we decided to take a winter vacation in Taiwan, the homeland picture in my mind became vivid and clear again. Everything there seemed wonderful. When the time to leave grew close, my husband and I were so eager to go back. We talked a lot about what to do, and even made a long restaurant list. More than that, I had dreams about going back as soon as we booked the tickets.

To be honest, the experience during the three weeks was not as good as we dreamed about. First of all, too many activities kept us from sleeping and recovering from jet lag. We were totally overwhelmed by the enthusiasm of our relatives and friends. My husband and I got very serious colds, I lost my voice at least one week and he got vertigo and spent four days in bed. We haven't been so sick for a long time. It seems that our bodies were totally relaxed and wanted to get some rest at that time.

Second, when I drove from the airport to my mother's house and neighborhood, my first impression was that it seemed small and crowed, neither graceful nor delicate. No driver would yield to pedestrians and walking on the streets seemed very dangerous, not to mention the air pollution. Moreover, the food was just ordinary and general. It was good, just as it should be, but not dreamlike. Everything was familiar but a little bit strange and distant.

One thing that surprised me most is about the ideas. I felt sad when I heard my friend let their kids stay at the babysitter's house or grandparents' during the weekday (just as I had done when I lived there). They only visited their kids or took them home on the weekend. Kids didn't get enough attention from adults and too much homework made them blue. They were unhappy and silent. This society I was familiar with has people who were too busy and had no family life. Then I knew I had changed a lot.

I think I am lucky because two years didn't change my homeland picture too much. It is still sweet as usual. But with this experience I won't idealize my homeland anymore and will cherish what I have now. But I know the days I am here will be another wonderful portion of the homeland memory in my life.

Questions for Reflection:

1. The author noticed that visiting her home country after having lived abroad highlighted some of the major cultural differences between the two places. Have you ever returned to a place after having been away from it for a long time? What surprised you? Were there both positive and negative surprises? Did that experience highlight any changes in yourself?

2. Think of a time you have adopted the value or behavior of a new culture (or subculture). What factors led to the change? How long had you been exposed to the new culture before the change occurred?

3. The author points out that in her culture it is common that "kids stay at the babysitter's house or grandparents' during the weekday" and are picked up by their parent only for the weekend. How does this compare to child-rearing/child care practices in your culture? What do these practices illustrate about cultural values?

Comment: page 157

Responsibility for Self-Management

It is about one year since I came to the USA. The most impressive and enlightening matter I have observed in the USA is the responsibility for self-management. Compared with Japanese, who think that hard work is the only way to live, Americans seem to live in comfort on the principle that enjoying life is most important and working is just a part of life. But I keenly realized that Americans have the responsibility to deal with everything on their own. Whether they can succeed in life or not depends on how they manage their lives. This principle applies to every aspect of life such as daily life, health, business, and education of children.

To take an instance in daily life, in America we have to check bills regularly, or we will be charged an unreasonable amount of money. I've been charged illegally more than one thousand dollars per month for my long distance calls by a company which I've neither made a contract with nor heard the name of. They dissolved the contract I had made with the other company, without any information or my permission, then they contracted with me without my permission. I've been obliged to spend a lot of time, energy, and patience in negotiating with the company to correct this mistake. After all that, they admitted their fault and I didn't have to pay any amount. It was very stupid, tough, and stressful for me, but I had to make every effort by myself not to lose anything.

On the other hand, in Japan, people seldom pay by check and the costs for daily living are generally withdrawn from their accounts automatically. However, such happenings mentioned above hardly ever occur in Japan. It bothers us Japanese, who are used to an automatic system, to have the responsibility to pay intensive and continuous attention to all bills.

In the field of health care, American women seem to be thorough in taking responsibility for periodic medical checks against breast and uterine cancer. Women in Japan are also asked to be responsible for the prevention against diseases, but few of them, many fewer than in America, take medical examinations independently. Even those who have a job and are forced to take examinations by the employers are always passive and reluctant to do so. Taken together, Americans seem to make every effort on their own to prevent disease and accidents before they occur.

Why do Americans take care of their health in such a different way from Japanese? The difference in the convenience of seeing a doctor between these two countries may be one reason. I always feel it is inconvenient to see a doctor in the USA, even with a slight cold or injury. In Japan we can easily see a medical specialist whom we like to consult without an appointment, even if we have a sudden serious illness. But it is not the case in the USA, which may make Americans more nervous in taking care of their health.

In summary, I realized how true it is that in the USA, nothing can pass comfortably in front of us without some independent attention being paid. I emphasize that in the USA we can never win the free and happy life in terms of money and health until we fulfill the responsibility for self-management.

Questions for Reflection:

1. Does any kind of telephone or utility fraud occur in your home country? Do you have to watch your bills carefully, or can you trust that they will be fair? How does medical screening occur in your home country? Is it up to you to make appointments for physical exams? Are any cultural values revealed in your answers to these questions?

2. Do you worry about your government having too much information about your private life, or would you prefer a government to have all the information it needs to help keep you safe and healthy? What does your answer reveal about your own cultural values?

3. Do you think that, basically, you have a lot of control over what happens to you in life, or do you think that mostly it is out of your hands?

Comment: page 158

Role of Shame in Parenting and Discipline

There have been a number of studies that describe the Japanese culture published in United States. Probably one of the most famous books is *The Chrysanthemum And the Sword: Patterns of Japanese Culture,* written by Ruth Benedict. Although it was published about 60 years ago, her precise explanation of the Japanese culture retains its interest today. In this classic book, she described the Japanese culture as "Culture of Haji (Shame)." On the other hand, she said there is more emphasis on "guilt" in the Western countries, which was probably originated from the Judeo-Christian idea that God knows everything and judges your every thought and deed. In Japan, one can think that one's behavior is based on, or dictated by, a sense of shame resulting from one's actions. Of course it doesn't mean that the Western culture is shameless, but Japanese place a great deal on the feeling of shame. The question here is: how does the idea affect our parenting?

When I was a child, I did a lot of bad things and didn't always follow our rules just like, I hope, many other children. My parents always said, "You should feel ashamed." I think it is somewhat different from "Shame on you," because the feeling of shame in Japan is an external feeling. In other words, you need others for feeling ashamed. "Others" are your neighbors, communities, or society.

For example, when my mother and I were in a toy store, I asked my mother to get something I wanted. When she refused, I started to cry and didn't want to leave the store. Then, my mother said, "Look! People are looking and laughing at us. We feel ashamed."

What does it mean? Why "we" not "you?" I think you should feel ashamed because you don't listen to your parent, and your mom should feel ashamed because she can't handle the situation. In this context, one could argue that it might be more important for Japanese not to be caught than not to feel ashamed. But my parents also told me that we should always behave as if others were looking at your every thought and deed. This is how we use the feeling of shame as a strong internal moral compass.

Another interesting example is that most Japanese parents want their children "not to trouble others" when they grow up. This is much more important to them than "to be respected by others." I would choose the first one as well, because I believe that this thought has already been imprinted in me; it is hard to get rid of. If you trouble others, they might think that you don't care about them very much. This is good enough for you to feel ashamed.

I think that parents in Japan spend a lot of time telling their children to behave well so that no one can blame them and their family, and not to trouble others. Otherwise, they feel ashamed. Now, let me ask you. What would you say to your child in a toy store?

Questions for Reflection:

1. How would most parents in your culture react to a child who demands something in a store that they do not want to buy? Try to imagine their actual words. Do these words teach children to pay attention to what others will think of them (shame) or to evaluate themselves internally (guilt)?

2. Which is more important to you — to not trouble others or to be respected by others?

3. Who should feel more shame in a toy store with a crying child — the child or the parent?

Comment: page 159

Starting a Friendship
with Americans in US

I think that starting a friendship in the US is not difficult for me, while starting a friendship with Americans in the US is not an easy task for me at all. As a matter of fact, since I arrived in Boston this January, I've made many friends from Taiwan, China, and Japan, but I've hardly had any American friends. For my personal experience, I attribute my difficulty of making friends with Americans to several reasons: English capability, culture differences, and the social network.

I suppose that the most important factor in starting a friendship with Americans in the US is English capability. With regard to my observation, I find that Americans tend to express their ideas by lots of talking and expect others to do the same. For example, my English teacher always tells me, "Say something, and don't be silent. Americans are not used to much silence." However, as a newcomer who is not a native English speaker, I need more patience and listening from others when getting along with American friends.

Secondly, I think cultural differences also play an important role in the course of making friends with Americans in the US. It goes without saying that people act differently when they make friends of different origins in different countries. For instance, in Taiwan, asking questions about one's marriage, job, and salary is very common and acceptable when people meet new friends, while those topics are not quite appropriate in the same situation in US. For another example, I grew up in a culture that puts much emphasis on modesty and listening. There is an old Chinese proverb saying, "Silence is gold." But in American I think the proverb should be, " Words are diamonds."

Additionally, I consider that the social network also has a major influence on making friends with Americans; this has been profound for me Because I suspended my busy occupation in Taiwan for one year in order to coordinate my husband's research in Boston, I came to the US and became a full-time housewife, which is a totally different life style for me. In the beginning of my first two months in Boston, aside from some Taiwanese housewives' gathering, my only social activity was my English class. Similarly, many of the classmates in my daytime English class were housewives from different countries, so that I was in an environment full of housewives from all over the world. We have shared many precious experiences about starting a new life in American, learning English, and cooking, but we didn't have any American friends with real local American experience. Then, I was admitted to a graduate school in my third month in Boston, and instantly I started to acquire some access to my American teachers, classmates, and staff of the school. Therefore, I will have more opportunity to start a friendship with Americans. My personal experience makes me learn about the importance of a social network in the course of starting a friendship with Americans. Finally, I think an open mind and an attempt to broaden one's social network both help me a lot in making the acquaintance of American friends.

Questions for Reflection:

1. What do you see as some main differences between individualist and collectivist conceptualizations of friendship? What are some other differences in the way friendship is conceptualized across different cultural contexts?

2. Have you ever tried to make friends with someone from a different culture? What was that experience like? Were you ever surprised or frustrated by the topics you and this friend would or would not discuss?

3. Think of the last time you made friends with someone from your home country — not a life-long friend, but a recent one. What was important to you about that friend — Shared interests? Shared experiences? Shared values?

Comment: page 160

Suing and Safety

Where Americans think of safety as the number one priority, Koreans think of the ability to work fast and efficiently as the first priority. And because of that, many accidents that should not have happened are happening frequently in Korea. I really envy the system in America: the way they deal with safety. However, this system of safety is quite often built on the goal of avoiding lawsuits, which means that people care a little more about safety because they don't want anyone to sue them. When I learned this, I began to look at the Americans' system of safety with a negative point of view.

Sometimes in a fast-food restaurant, I buy a cup of coffee. As I scan the disposable cup I look for something I hope not to find. It is the sign that says, "Caution. Hot!" I am disappointed whenever I see that stupid sign for adults. Yes, of course, the hot water can burn people. Kids as well as adults know better than to be careless with hot water. Of course I know the reason why the company put that sign on the disposable cup. It is to avoid being sued when someone accidentally burns him or herself. This reason brought a negative point of view into my mind. But as time went on, I learned that suing helps people protect themselves from many dangerous problems when they have an accident.

Some time ago, one of my friends fell in front of her rented house in the US, and was carried to the hospital. The water from her roof had dripped down to the front of the house, creating a pack of slippery ice right in front of her house. It wasn't a huge accident, but it was hard for her to sit down, or even to walk. The hospital could not cure her, so she had to go to the oriental clinic to be treated. It cost a lot of money. When she told the apartment management office about this accident, the office replied that they already had insurance prepared for this kind of incident that would pay for her costs. It was just surprising. They had insurance prepared for this kind of incident! Korean apartments have an office, but don't handle these kinds of accidents. From my friend's case, I learned that suing gives people more ability to protect themselves. Also, I learned that many rules concerning safety are made to help the people in these matters. This was an accident that changed my point of view about suing.

In Korea, suing is not common. We handle little matters with the neighbors instead of going to court. We talk and sometimes fight with the neighbors over some problems. Therefore, the system of suing was unfamiliar to me. Naturally, I have little understanding about suing. But if that system of suing brings the value of safety back into life in Korea, I would be glad for the system to be used in Korea. It might be true that suing makes people aware of the safety of other people and that it makes them obey the rules more. I think it is not important to decide whether suing is more important than safety. I think it is more important that people can be protected from many dangers they might face. From these points, I think it is important for Americans to make a system where they think of the safety of the people above all other things, and to keep this system going. On the other hand, I think it is important for us Koreans to learn this kind of system from the Americans.

Questions for Reflection:

1. What happens in your home country if a person falls down in front of their rented home? Is the owner responsible to ensure that there is no danger around the house? What cultural values or beliefs are highlighted by your response?

2. The author points out that suing and safety are more common in the US than in her culture. What cultural beliefs/values does this illustrate in each cultural context?

3. Which system do you prefer, a more safety-oriented or a more speed- and efficiency-oriented approach? Why?

Comment: page 161

The Word You Won't See in a Dictionary

Since I have lived in a foreign country for many years, I know that you learn language through experience. Even if I consult a dictionary for words which I do not understand, there are some that are not described in a dictionary. Although American parents teach their children about words they should not use, it is difficult for parents who are in the US temporarily to understand and teach their children about words that are considered vulgar.

One day the daughter of one of my Japanese friends joined the Girl Scouts. The girl's family has been in the US over 8 years. For her, nothing was problematic with English. The girl was writing a note about the schedule for the group meeting. When the meeting finished and the girl submitted the paper with her notes, the counselor got angry and made a terrible face. "Who has written this?" he said in an angry voice. The director and many persons gathered around them. The Japanese's girl raised her hand honestly, saying, "I took the notes." But she did not understand why the adults would get angry with her. The child had made notes of the schedule on the paper. The counselor asked her, "Did you also write this word?" The girl answered honestly, "Yes, I wrote it." She had used the so-called "language which is not good." She was asked by the counselor, "Why did you write it?" The girl answered, "I was the person in charge who took notes from the meeting. I listened to these words used in the group. However, I put it down because I did not understand the meaning of these words," she explained. The counselor telephoned her parents, without being convinced. But the child truly did not know the meaning. She had not been taught by her parents about this word.

I got very interested in this kind of talk because my daughter did not know the meaning of the same word, either. She did not know the meaning of some words that a friend uses occasionally in school. My daughter asked her friend about the meaning. However, the friend looked at her face very incredulously. "Are you lying? Do you really not know this meaning?" The friend was really surprised that my daughter did not know the meaning. In addition, the friend said, "She knows nothing" to another friend. "She does not know the meaning of this language." The other friends giggled.

The friend said, "If you don't understand, why don't you ask your parents?" My daughter did not understand why everybody would laugh and giggle. But she guessed that it had a bad meaning from everybody's expression and attitude. Therefore, she didn't want to consult her parents. She consulted a dictionary. Although the meaning was written in the dictionary, she did not understand from it why everybody was laughing, because in the dictionary the definition was written carefully, using appropriate expressions. I thought that my daughter was feeling that the definition in the dictionary did not match her friend's reaction.

I feel like there are a lot of things that we can't learn from a dictionary in an ordinary day. A foreign child has a lot of expressions that a parent is not taught. They must experience it and must understand it. Then they grow up in that way.

Questions for Reflection:

1. Has anything like this happened to you — have you ever been taken by surprise by a cultural or language mistake?

2. How do children learn which words not to use in your home country? Why didn't that work for these two girls?

3. What kinds of words are not appropriate to use in the US? What is different between how adults who are learning a second language and children who are learning a second language learn this lesson?

4. If you were in a situation like the writer, would you have someone you could ask about the meaning of the word your daughter used? How trusted must a

friend or teacher be before asking such a question, in your mind?

5. Think of a time you had to learn an unwritten rule, or a rule about some socially unacceptable behavior. How did you learn you were in dangerous territory? Did someone explain it to you or did you encounter negative reactions? How did you learn what to do?

Comment: page 163

Customs

Barrier-Free

Have you ever heard the term "barrier-free?" I said to an American friend that nowadays the barrier-free style has spread widely in Japan, especially when we Japanese build a house. But the American friend didn't understand what that term meant. He said, "What is 'barrier-free?' I've never heard the word." I wondered because the word is obviously in English. Another friend explained that is Janglish, or Japanese-English. So, I explained the meaning to him – that it means getting rid of barriers that are an obstruction to elderly, disabled people, and pregnant women, for example reducing level differences and slopes, or smoothing road surfaces.

However, you may be surprised when you are in Japan. For example, think about bathroom style. When I had just arrived in America I stopped by a small noodle shop to have lunch and I used the bathroom that was huge, given that the shop only had a few seats, so that I was impressed. There was a handrail and a supporting bar in there and I was reminded, "Here is America." Every bathroom has a big stall for people who are handicapped or elderly. We Japanese are absolutely certain that we are becoming an aging society, with numbers of elderly people of 65 years or older growing very quickly. As they age, elderly people suffer a decline in their walking ability and their physical strength. But the conveniences are not adequate for them. I expect that big stalls for these people will be set up widely in our society.

Or consider sidewalks, roads and parking spaces. The space that wheelchair users and visually impaired people can use easily is clearly valued in America. For example there are provisions for guaranteeing adequately wide pedestrian space, reducing big curb differences, smoothing road surfaces, and making crosswalks safer, so that all pedestrians, including elderly and disabled people, can use roads safely. We Japanese must develop public awareness about parking access that is below the norm, both because there are not enough spaces anywhere and because they are used by thoughtless people.

The third thing is how people treat others who are different. It is difficult to explain, but I could describe one episode. When I visited Japan during summer vacation, I went to a small shop to buy goods and I was waiting in a line to pay. There were some people before me and I found a person who was a wheelchair user waiting in front of the register. The line was going on but nobody asked him anything.

My turn came around and I asked him, "You can go first." He said in a small voice, "No, thank you." I asked again, "If you'd like, please go ahead."

"My hand doesn't work. I can't put items on the counter and can't pay without help, but my helper is attending another person now, so I am waiting for her to come back to help me," he said. His hand was bent and suspended from a wire on the chair.

"What can I do for you, may I help somehow?" I said. "Can you put my items on the counter and open my purse then? Could you pay for them instead of me?" he said.

"My pleasure, but is that OK if I open your purse?" I asked. "I'd be grateful if you would," he said. But I wavered a little bit because this was the first time to open a purse for a person I met for the first time in a shop. The cashier gazed at our conversation and just stood in front of us. When I opened his purse I asked again and again, "Is this OK, I will pay one, two, and three thousand yen. ...Here is the change...100, 200, 300 and ....yen. " Then I put the goods in his bag. Suddenly his helper came and she said she was sorry to make him wait. He really appreciated what I did and explained that to the helper. They bowed over and over again and he said to me, "I'm sorry." "I'm sorry," the helper said too.

"It's fine, OK, OK fine! Take care," I stammered because my head was filled with wonder. Why did they think of "sorry?" Why was I told "sorry?" Why was the employee just standing and gazing at him? Why couldn't I say, "You are welcome?"

I really know we Japanese often say "sorry" without any big meaning, as if in a greeting. However, to be honest, my feeling was not pleasant because I realized he might have hesitated to say what he wanted to anybody around him. He might be shy. But I comprehended that there was an unseen barrier in which the person in a wheelchair thinks of saying "sorry" rather than "thank you," and that this has become like a law between each other in our society. In America, they don't say "sorry," they say "thank you" naturally at such occasions.

The accessible society will be coming in the near future. Now in Japan to be prepared for aging society, it is becoming common to offer a barrier-free housing style However how has recognition changed in our society? This quality of public awareness is the issue that we have to improve. "I hope that we will give further momentum to any promotion for barrier-free environments in the society." These are the words our prime minister addressed and we hope to have barrier-free environments in days to come soon.

Questions for Reflection:

1. How do provisions for people with disabilities or elderly people in your home country compare to those in the US?

2. Would a person with a disability in your home country be more likely to say "sorry" or "thank you," in a situation like this? Why ? What does your answer reveal about cultural values?

3. The author discusses "how people treat others who are different" in two cultural contexts. How are "people who are different" generally perceived in your culture? What might that indicate about cultural values?

Comment: page 164

Birthday Parties

My daughters (a third grader and a first grader) have been invited to their classmates' birthday parties three times. One daughter went to a slumber party (with her own sleeping bag) at her classmate's home. The other has been invited twice. One was at a classmate's house, and the other was at the local Aquarium. I let her go to the first one but not the second.

I was impressed by the party that my younger daughter went to. There were lots of decorations, balloons, toys, cookies, cakes and other desserts, and so on. I was sure everyone had fun. I appreciated the fact that the host family gave my daughter a wonderful experience. But there was something that surprised me. When I picked her up, she had a bag of goodies with her. When we got home I noticed that she had a new pair of socks on. Later I found out that they were beating a piñata at the party, and the floor got sticky. The parents of the birthday girl gave every guest a new pair of socks as a result.

I think many parents here spend too much money and time for kids' birthday parties. Here are my questions.

1) Is it common for people to throw birthday parties?

2) Are birthday parties for kids common?

3) Do the adults who hold birthday parties for their kids do the same for their own parents?

4) Is it a good thing for children to invite so many people to help celebrate their birthdays?

5) What is the true meaning or purpose of a birthday party?

6) If I receive a birthday invitation along with my daughters, should I mail a birthday card? Also, if I send my kids to the party, what kind of gift would be a good choice? How much would an ideal present cost? In addition, should I buy an expensive present for a slumber party, but a cheaper one for a 2-hour party?

7) If the presents that my daughters bring to a party are inexpensive, but they bring home expensive things, what should I do? Should I buy another gift?

8) Are birthday parties really necessary or expected?

I am not against birthday parties, and I can certainly come up with a list of good things about such parties. But to me personally a birthday is just a number, and why should we celebrate a number? Is the birthday cake the point? Or the birthday wishes? Or the fun? I don't know. To me, instead of a party to celebrate my birthday, it is more important to say "thanks" to my mother for bringing me to the world and raising me.

Questions for Reflection:

1. Answer the author's questions, from your own experience. How would you answer them about your home culture? How might you answer them from the perspective of other cultures you have experienced or studied? What do you think about the expenditure of time and money on birthday parties for children?

2. Did you grow up having birthday parties like what the American ones described here? Have you seen or had parties like this for your, or others' children? Birthday parties put the spotlight on an individual child for a moment. Does that seem like a good idea to you? What values (positive and negative) do you think parents are teaching their children through such parties?

3. Do you think it is a good thing for a child to have a lot of attention, one day a year? What about a lot of gifts? If there could be a birthday party in which a child was the center of attention but received no gifts, what would you think? Would this address the author's (or other collectivists') concerns, or not? If this kind of party became a community norm, would that better or worse, from your point of view?

4. Do you celebrate birthdays in your culture/family? If so, how? Do you know of any variations in how birthdays are observed (or not) in families or cultures you are familiar with? What do these variations in birthday observations reveal about a culture's values? What are the most significant celebrations in your culture? Why do you think they are valued? Would you say these celebrations focus more on individuals or on families or other groups? What does this say about your cultural values?

5. Have you ever adopted a custom from a new culture? How was it different from what you did in your home culture? How did the new custom make you feel?

Comment: page 165

The Culture of Dumping

Garbage has always been a problem in Korea. With its narrow land and its ever-growing population, the Korean government has tried to solve this problem by making key decisions to help.

The Korean government decided somewhat expensively to sell specific plastic bags for garbage (except for recyclable things) that were labeled with the city's name. If people were caught using other bags for garbage to put at the dumping ground, they had to pay a fine. We pay for garbage collection depending on the number and size of bags. This system helps people reduce their amount of garbage. The government also asked the supermarkets to charge their customers for the bags they used to pack bought goods. This discouraged the use of new plastic bags and encouraged the re-use of plastic bags, which can be pollutants.

I remember my first trip to the supermarket in the United States. I was shocked to find the worker packing my food with such a large number of plastic bags. I was worried that I would actually have to pay more for them because I was so used to paying for them in Korea. I also was surprised by the large quantity, as well as the various types, of disposable goods that were in great abundance in the American supermarkets (for example, paper cups and plates, and zip-lock bags). In Korea, the government has discouraged the use of such products because the materials they were made out of include plastic or foam, all of which are hard to dispose of.
America as a whole is interested in recycling. For example, several hotels here send out recommendations to their customers asking them to reuse their bed sheets so that hotels could contribute to the reduction of water pollution. By seeing this happen, I realized that the difference between Korea and America is that recycling in America is voluntary, while in Korea it is enforced in a more direct and forceful fashion. For the time being, this was necessary in Korea because the garbage problem had gotten so bad. Korean lack of land makes it hard to find the proper place to dump garbage. In spite of this difference of natural resources, it's natural that both Korea and America need to contribute as a whole to the effort of keeping natural.

Questions for Reflection:

1. In Korea, people are required to buy trash bags and plastic shopping bags as part of a government initiative to consider the environment and reduce waste. How do these initiatives compare to those in your country?

2. Have you noticed a difference in wastefulness of any type between the US and other countries? What cultural values do you think shape these differences?

3. What obstacles to environmental change exist in your home country? That is, what, if anything, makes it hard for people to recycle and use few resources?

4. How do you think US Americans might react to government initiatives such as those described here?

Comment: page166

Family Advice about Pregnancy

I had my first baby in the US seventeen years ago. In the Chinese way of counting age, my son is eighteen years old now, because a baby's age is calculated from the beginning of pregnancy, not the date of the baby's birth. So I am confused about my kids' age sometimes.

When I found out I was pregnant back seventeen years ago, the first thought that came to my mind was the coming baby's gender. Chinese families regard the males' role to keep the family blood line; besides, my husband is the only son in his family. As I was the one to deliver a baby, it seemed that I had full responsibility to have a son to keep this blood line even though my husband and I both know the fact that a baby's gender is not decided by me. I would like a girl baby very much, but to relieve the burden of this great responsibility, I would rather have a son first.

Chinese people always say, "She has happiness" instead of "She is pregnant." Of course, my family was so pleased to hear that "I had happiness," especially my mother. She kept telling me a lot of rules for the pregnancy. Furthermore, she gave the rules for *zho-yeh-tz* which, in Chinese culture, means the mother is required to stay in bed for a month to recover when the baby is born. In this month, I was advised to stay at home, not go outdoors and avoid cold, wind, dirty air, ice, and cold drinks. The most serious rule for me was not to take a shower or wash my hair for this period of time.

After 9 months of waiting, I finally had a baby boy. Right after my baby was delivered; I asked the nurse for some water, she gave me some ice cubes. I had to break the rules my mother told me because I was thirsty. Then the nurse suggested that I walk to the room, which was also prohibited by the rules of staying in bed right after the baby was born. I had to keep this rule because I couldn't walk at that time. Instead, I asked for a wheel chair. When I got to the room, I was happy and relaxed. I remembered the rules for *zho-yeh-tz* and kept staying in bed, without taking a shower and washing my hair for the first day. The nurse came the next day and found out that all the towels in my bathroom were unused. I could see her face showing a kind of confusion. She asked me to get down and helped me to do a little exercise. Right after I got out of the bed, I blacked out. Thereafter, I messed up the towels purposely so the nurse would not have to worry anymore, and so I could also keep the rules at the same time.

I believe this situation happens in Taiwan in the opposite way. In order to keep the culture, although all those mothers-to-be keep promising to do the *zho-yeh-tz* so their mothers-in-law will be satisfied, they sometimes do not obey the rule by taking a shower, washing their hair and drinking something cold sneakily.

Questions for Reflection:

1. Have you been in situations where you were expected to participate in customs that you felt uncomfortable with? How did you manage those situations?

2. What are the childbirth customs in your culture?

3. Have you ever broken any "cultural rules?" What was that like? How did others react?

4. Are there any cultural rules/norms that are important to you that you have chosen not to break even though others are unfamiliar or confused by them?

5. Whose advice about parenting and health care do you take seriously – Your parents? Your parents-in-law? Your grandparents? Would it be easy or difficult to ignore their advice? What if they were not there to see you ignore them?

Comment: page 167

Feet on the Seat

Since the time I have been here in the United States, I have noticed so many differences between Taiwan and US. One thing surprising me is that some people like to put their feet on the back of the seat in front of them in theaters. By my observation, it seems to be the American way. However, it is not allowed in Taiwan since it is not polite or good looking and the seat would get dirty. In Taiwan, if you put your feet on the front seat, the theater staff would stop you from doing it.

After I experienced this event here, I had some doubts in my mind. Is it really fitting to put your feet on the seat in a theater in US? What would you do while people put their feet on your seat? I tried hard to figure this event out.

One day, I went to the Shubert Theater to see a dance show with my family. There were four students sitting behind our seats. All of them put their feet on our seats. Although the feet didn't touch our body, it made me feel upset and bad. The student just behind my husband let her feet touch his back during the show time. However, my husband didn't say anything about it. She put her feet on my husband's seat till the end of the show. In truth, I don't feel good when people put their feet on my seat. After we went home I discussed this behavior with my children because they also wanted to mimic this behavior in that time. I asked them not to do it based on the traditional Chinese culture. On the other hand I worry that they will do it since their classmates or friends act like this when I cannot accompany them.

Questions for Reflection:

1. Do people in your home country put their feet on the seat in front of them in a theater or stadium? Is this an accepted practice? How would you feel if someone behind you put his/her feet on your seat?

2. What are some other examples of informality in the US? How would you compare US Americans' level of formality to other cultures? What are some examples of formality or informality in your culture?

3. People often feel uncomfortable when norms about proximity are broken. It is easy to blame such discomfort on personality traits of the other person ("aggressive" or "flirtatious") rather than on cultural norm differences. What are the norms about proximity in your culture? For example, when having a conversation with a friend or colleague, how far apart would you typically stand? Has anyone ever broken your social norms when it comes to proximity? That is, has anyone ever stood too close for comfort or too far for comfort? What was your reaction?

4. The author informed her children not to engage in a behavior that she perceives as "normal" in the US context but quite inappropriate in a Chinese context. For her, it is important that her children retain certain Chinese values, in this case the value regarding Chinese conceptualizations of politeness. What do you think it is like for both children and adults to negotiate social and cultural norms between the two cultures? What are the benefits and challenges of this experience?

Comment: page 168

Gift Giving in Return

My friends recently gave me a baby shower. I thought about giving a gift to them in return. In Japan, we give gifts in return after almost every celebration (for weddings, graduations, getting a job and even funerals). That is, if we get a gift, we have to give a gift back to the person who gave us one. It should cost one-half of the price of the gift we received. We call the custom "Han-gaeshi" in Japanese; it means a half return.

I think this Japanese custom comes from Japanese hesitation and modesty. We feel sorry that we owe somebody something. Actually, I don't like it because it is ridiculous and it tends to give and take forever. Sometimes it hurts the person who prepares the gift.

This time, I decided to give a chocolate with a thank you card. Of course, my American friends were a little bit surprised when I gave a gift to them in return. I had to explain the Japanese custom and the meaning: I gave them sweets because we wanted to share our sweet thankful feeling. But I was not sure they understood this meaning.

Questions for Reflection:

1. In your home culture, are gifts given before a baby is born? at weddings? birthdays? graduations? funerals? holidays?

2. Do bosses give gifts to their staff or do employees give gifts to their bosses? Why do you think this is? What cultural values are revealed by these practices?

3. Does your home culture have rules about gift-giving – who should get a gift, how much it should cost, whether to wrap it, whether to open it in the presence of the giver, etc? Are these rules strict or flexible?

4. Would you feel surprised to get a "half return" gift from someone you had given a gift to, or would you expect it?

5. How do you (and people in your home culture) feel when someone has done something nice for you? Under what circumstances would you take action to eliminate a sense of obligation rather than just be grateful? Can you think of an example of each?

Comment: page 169

Golden Week

In Japan, we have many national holidays from the end of April to the beginning of May. We call this "Golden Week." Many Japanese take paid vacations on the intervening work days. Some companies close completely and give employees time off. Golden Week is one of the longest vacation periods in Japan. Many people travel around the country or abroad, so many sightseeing and amusement places are very crowded at this time. In addition to Golden Week, we have two other vacations which may also be observed for most of the week: "Oshogatsu" (New Year's Day) in January and "Obon" in August. Many places and transportation are very crowded in these periods, too.

After I came to the US, I was surprised to learn that some holidays are different in each state, and at each work place. While the US has 10 national holidays, we have 15 national holidays in Japan. On the other hand, average paid time off is about 9 days in Japan, and 13 days in the US.

I've read that many Japanese hesitate to take a vacation unless everybody in their workplace will take a vacation at the same time, and that is the reason why there are so many national holidays in Japan.

Questions for Reflection:

1. Every country has holidays, but not every country observes holidays for a week or more at a time. Are there weeks in your home country when most people do not work? Do they tend to travel and take vacation on these days? Are vacation spots very crowded on any particular weeks?

2. What are the advantages to a business of everyone taking vacation at the same time? What are the disadvantages?

3. Consider that there are 10 national holidays and an average of 13 paid vacation days in the US compared with 15 national holidays and an average of 9 paid vacation days in Japan. How many national holidays are celebrated in your country? What is the average amount of paid vacation days?

4. The author also points out that many people in her culture do not feel comfortable taking time off from work unless everybody else is also taking time off. What does this tell us about the values of her culture? How would you compare those values to those of your own culture?

Comment: page 171

Korean Daughter-in-Law

One of the differences between the US and Korea is that, while Americans put much value on individuality, Koreans emphasize community. I am always aware that I live as a member of a family, school or country, not just as "myself." We get accustomed to using the word "our" instead of "my." "To do your best in everything for the fame of our family." "Study hard, and our class will be the first in the exam." We are all raised to be reminded of our responsibilities as a member: as a daughter, as a student, and as a sister. As a result, I always bear various duties in mind. That means I can't do many things at my own will, because others, like parents, teachers, and friends, are already expecting me to do things in a certain way. Because of these expectations, the lives of young women in Korea are more similar than they are in America.

We have a custom for married daughters to belong to their husband's families. Therefore, I should do my duty, which was taught by my parents and came from the Confucian teaching, and become a member of my husband's family. So, I was supposed to respect my parents-in-law and get along with the other daughters-in- law and relatives. So, I did call them twice a week to say hello, visit them and stay for a few days on important holidays and celebrate their birthday with many foods and quite expensive presents.

Because next year is my father-in-law's 70th birthday, which has an important meaning for Koreans, I have saved a certain amount of money for him for 10 years with other two daughters-in-law. Now, it amounts to $10,000. We will give it to him and he will be pleased, not because of the amount of money, but because of the concern by the children. Furthermore, someday, it will be our charge to take them to the hospital and care for them. I think that is my duty, and, at the same time, the duty of all our Korean daughters-in-law.

I am sure it is definitely right for the children to thank their parents for bringing them up and to repay the obligation which parents gave. So, it is nice for the daughter-in-law, as a new daughter, to do good for the parents-in-law, who become weak and may feel isolated from others. Nevertheless, it is true that to be so involved in many family things is a burden for the daughter-in-law. On holidays, most daughters-in-law spend three to four days in their parents-in-law's kitchen to make food. We also might spend a lot of energy thinking about the relationships between members of the family. Moreover, many women think it is not fair for daughters-in-law to do more things for their parents-in-law than their own parents. Who can take care of her parents if they don't have a son?
Even though we complain about family things and the custom, there is one thing that can't be changed and is agreed by every Korean. It is that children should respect either their parents or parents-in-law. We can't return their favors forever no matter how much we try.

Questions for Reflection:

1. In your family, is it very clear who is expected to take care of the elderly parents, aunts and uncles and grandparents? If so, is this expectation based on gender and birth order (for example, the "eldest male" or "youngest daughter")? If not, how is it decided who will do this care?

2. Do you agree that children have an obligation to re-pay their parents for bringing them up? Or do you identify more with the individualistic concept of how adult children and parents should relate to each other? Thinking beyond your own family to society in general, do you think the answer to this question depends on how "good a job" the parent did, or is there an obligation of loyalty

regardless of the quality of the parent-child relationship?

3. What would your father-in-law's reaction be to a gift of $10,000 from his daughters-in-law (or, how do you think the typical father-in-law would react to such a gift in your culture?)? Surprise? Pride? Shame? What values are revealed in your answer to this question?

4. In your experience, thinking of your own and your friends' families, do people in your culture tend to take on the kind of obligation and loyalty to family elders described here? How is it similar and how is it different?

Comment: page 171

Play Dates

I'd like to introduce the Japanese play date style. In Japan, mothers don't have to accompany their children who are elementary students when they go to school, their friends' houses, or parks. Usually the mothers know the areas and the houses where they might go, and make sure they come back home at a certain time, around 5:00. At the park, they can always find friends. And then, they often go to the house of one child without arrangement. Sometimes, especially in summer, several of my son's friends might suddenly come into my house with my son while playing outside, shouting, "I'm thirsty!" "I'm hungry," with dirty hands, feet, and clothes. And they play at my house for a while. It's a common scene.

Sometimes during school time, children promise each other to play together at someone's house. In this case, the mothers call the friend's mother to ask if it's convenient for her or not. If it's all right, they send the children with a small gift like a snack food. It is very common that more than two children gather at a house.

They are very free. But they have to work out their problems by themselves, for example being mean or ignoring. Sometimes they have serious problems, but it might be training to cooperate in settling the problems. In Japan, we often say, "Adults should not interfere in children's arguments or fights." (Japanese mothers usually intervene in children's fights if it's serious.) Japanese children learn how to behave between friends by playing without adults' interfering.

This is the Japanese style. I think we can have this custom in Japan for three reasons. First, suburbs are very safe. Secondly, communities are small, so children can reach their friends easily on foot or by bicycle. Thirdly, we are almost homogeneous, and have similar cultural values, history, and expectations, so we can easily understand each other. So it's reasonable that there are differences in play dates between US and Japan. But I have one question for US American parents. Why isn't it common that three or four children have a play date?

Questions for Reflection:

1. Think about how you played with other children when you were growing up. Did parents arrange and supervise the play? Were you usually in small or larger groups? What cultural values do you think you learned in those play situations?

2. If you overheard your own children arguing with each other, would you intervene to help them settle their differences? What would most people in your home country do? What if they were your neighbor's children, not yours? Strangers' children? What, if any thing, would make you more likely to do or say something?

3. Do you agree that "adults should not interfere in children's arguments or fights." Why or why not? What cultural values or lessons does this approach to managing conflict promote?

4. What are the advantages of living in a community where people have similar backgrounds and values? What are the advantages of living in a community where people come from very different backgrounds and values?

Comment: page 173

Receiving Visitors

We are filled with joy at meeting a new friend. Most children meet friends of their age in the same classroom or on the playground. As they play and do something together, they become close friends. The next step is probably inviting friends to their home. People tend to like showing their own room and toys to their friends. It is a suitable way to know each other. Most Korean children pride themselves on having many friends who want to come to their house. Visiting and inviting others is more natural and easier in Korea than in the US. In Korea, it is common to invite people over for tea or lunch, even though they are not close friends. It is not always necessary to call or make an appointment before visiting. Sometimes we get greater joy when we have visitors without prior notice.

When guests visit us, we treat them as well as we can. We are also hospitable toward unexpected guests. Treating guests well is our way of being polite as well as our duty in Korea. We make them feel as comfortable as in their own home. We express our concern about the visitors and their work and ask how their families are doing. Americans also make their guests welcome in many ways — by body language and words.

Furthermore, we serve the most delicious food that we have. Even if the food is not expensive, we take great care in serving it. Sometimes, visitors suffer when they have to eat something served even though they are not hungry. We regard it as polite to eat whether we are hungry or not. The host feels satisfied when their guests say they have enjoyed the food, so we are sorry if we don't have anything special to serve. It is the same whether the visitor is a child or a grown-up. Anybody who comes to my home is asked what he wants to drink, or if he is hungry. I think it is one of the most beautiful aspects in Korean culture.

My son was once invited to his American friend's home after school.

As soon as my son came back home, he shouted, "Mom, I'm hungry." At this remark I was very surprised. I couldn't understand why he was hungry. "Haven't you had any thing in his house?" I asked. "Just a little chip," he answered. I thought he wouldn't be hungry because he had been treated well. It was his first visit to his friend in the US. When his friend came to my house after that, I put some fruit, chips, and juice on the table. Seeing the table, my son asked, "Don't do that. Not too much in the US." I acknowledged how different it was from my country. Not serving sufficient food was an unthinkable, unimaginable situation.

In fact, children understandably have no time to eat anything because they are busy playing. I heard that people don't eat much before dinner and parents are concerned about their children's weight in the US. I heard it is usual not to serve tea to visitors. If visitors ask, it will be served. Of course, it depends on the family, and on whether the visitors are close friends or not and whether they come with an appointment or not. In our case, we usually serve a non-alcoholic drink when a repairman visits us. It is no wonder that it is our traditional custom to treat visitors with food. Serving food to guests is very important in my country, but our focus is not on entertaining with others, but rather on having interesting in discussion, games and so on.

It seems to be an insignificant difference, but it is big to me. I have appreciated that the attitude to treat visitors is quite different in two cultures.

Questions for Reflection:

1. In your home country, would you expect a school-age playmate to be offered a snack by the host parent, or would you expect the playmate guest to ask for what he/she wants?

2. Do you offer a drink or food to the repairmen who come to your house in your home country? How do you think this varies in other cultural contexts?

84

3. The author points out that her child was trying to fit in with the US American way of doing things. Have you ever observed yourself or a child trying to fit in with new way of doing things, even if you/they don't really prefer it? What would have to change for you to behave in the way you prefer?

Comment: page 174

Slumber Party

I've never had a slumber party in my life. "Sleeping over" at someone's house is an odd idea and hard to imagine! So when I got the parent's phone call that she wanted to invite my daughter to have a slumber party with four other girls in her house, I just didn't know how to respond. Luckily, I know her very well, I could trust her, so I told her right away: "I'll make some dumplings for you, then you don't need to cook a lot!"

A slumber party does not just mean sleeping over in a friend's house; it also means that the host has to be responsible to take care of others' girls! I was wondering if American moms have nothing to do? Or is there really lots of fun that I never experienced?

When I was 10, my neighbor asked me to sleep over in her house because her father was out of town and her mother thought that it would be a good idea to let two girls sleep together. So when I asked my father: "Could I sleep over at Geng's house?" my father just stared at me with his big eyes and said angrily: "Is there no bed for you in our own house?" Later I figured out that my father thought that well-behaved girls never sleep over outside, that it's inappropriate to bother other people to take care of one's own child.

My father's look was so strong that I couldn't forget it and never asked him to sleep over again until I became a sophomore. I lived in a dormitory of my college at that time. Lots of college students preferred to rent a space off campus instead of living in the dormitory. I envied my friends because they could stay out late in the café to discuss interesting topics, while I had to rush back to my dormitory before 10 o'clock. So I encouraged myself and wrote a letter to my father to try to get his permission to move out of the dormitory. My father was so cool that he didn't say yes or no, he didn't even give me a word; instead he sent me an article that had been cut from the newspaper, the title was: Sophomore Who Lived Off Campus Was Raped at her Apartment. Obviously, my father's answer was NO!

If I had never lived in America, then there would be 99% possibility for me to follow my father's steps and forbid my daughters to sleep over at their friend's house. Chinese people dislike bothering other people. Thinking about a slumber party, you have to prepare the dinner and breakfast, share the room, and take turns to use the bathroom, rent a movie or get some funny game to let them indulge. If they are too young, they might need your help or call you all the time! When they leave, you need to clean the house. It's hard work, isn't it? Even harder than taking care of my own girls.

But I did, I had a slumber party for my daughters last week. And I found out that there was really something in there! It offered me a chance to observe how they interact. To know much about my own girls, and to know more about the friends they are making now! The most important part was I could tell one of the girls wasn't so comfortable and the other just perfectly fit in my house. And this is the part that I am curious about most. Because I hope my daughters can feel comfortable and relaxed while they are staying with their friends. I hope my girls can feel at ease no matter under what kind of situation. That kind of personality can be built, right?

So I do appreciate the parents who invited my girls to sleep over. For that reason, I am willing to do anything to help them reduce their hard work such as making lots of dumplings. This is all I can do.

Questions for Reflection

1. Do children have slumber parties/sleepovers with other children in your home country? If not, how would this concept sound there? Would people respond like the author's father?

2. In your home culture, would hosting a sleepover for children feel like a burden for most parents? Would they do anything different because a guest was there?

3. In your home culture, whom can you "burden" or inconvenience? Whom can you ask for help – for example, to pick up a package for you at a post office, or to watch your children while you go to a doctor's appointment? A spouse? A sibling? A parent? A neighbor? A friend? How well do you have to know someone before asking for such things?

4. How can parents or teachers prepare children to be flexible in different situations?

5. Think of a time you have adopted the value or behavior of a new national or organizational culture. What factors led to the change? How long had you been exposed to the new culture before the change occurred?

6. One doesn't have to move to a new culture to change one's mind about a value or belief. Can you think of a sequence like that described in this story, from your life, when you slowly examined a deeply-held belief, then tried out something quite different? What led you to try out the new way?

Comment: page 176

Two Thoughts about Babysitting

When I worked in Japan, our children went to daycare from eight to four o'clock. Sometimes I had a meeting in the early morning, and if my husband couldn't take care of our children, we asked my parents, who lived near our house, to help us. Actually, we decided to live near my parents' house, because we expected lots of their help. Usually, I came back home (to my parents' home) around seven to nine o'clock. My mother picked up our children from daycare and prepared the dinner. If I came back later, we stayed that night at my parents' home.

When I talked about my job and life-style in Japan to my American friends, they were very surprised. My American friends said they ask a baby-sitter at first in that case. Some of them asked me, "Did you pay your parents?" Of course, I didn't. It's not only me who asks parents to baby-sit in Japan. Many of my friends who worked with me rely on daycare and parents. It is common that the grandparents (or sometimes other relatives) help take care of the grandchildren in Japan and we don't have an idea to pay for it. We prefer to ask our parents rather than a stranger. And when the first child becomes older (like middle grader), he/she has responsibility for the younger siblings.

In America, we can't leave children at home by themselves. Since last summer, we finally found a Japanese baby-sitter and asked her to baby-sit several times. My American friends showed pleasure to hear this news, and asked me whether I went out to dinner with my husband or not. This thinking didn't occur in my mind before, because I felt guilty to my children when I asked others to watch them. I also have some worries about the baby-sitting. So, I ask for baby-sitting only when I have business and it is necessary by all means. Maybe this is the culture difference and I'm not used to the American style. (My husband said he has no guilty feeling because for the children, it is the same thing that the baby-sitter watches them for any reason!) I really would like to go to dinner without my children, but I think I have to wait till my youngest one becomes bigger and my children are used to the baby-sitter.

Questions for Reflection:

1. In your home culture, how do most people feel about leaving their children with babysitters or in child care? Do you agree with this view? Why or why not? What does this custom reveal about broader cultural norms and values?

2. What is your reaction to the author's description of feeling guilty when leaving her children with a babysitter? What does your reaction teach you about what you value?

3. Whom do you include when you list the people in your "family?" Did you include siblings, aunts, uncles, cousins, and grandparents, or only your nuclear family? What does this reveal about your cultural values?

4. Is it common for grandparents to take care of grandchildren in your home country?

5. Is it common for spouses to go to a social event together, without children, in your home culture? What does this reveal about your home's cultural values?

6. Can you think of an example when you had to do something differently, repeatedly, in a new country compared to how you behaved in your home country? Did your ideas or values change, or not?

7. What are the benefits to a society of children being raised and tended only by their parents and close family members? What are the benefits to a society of children being tended occasionally by an outsider? Are there downsides to either?

Comment: page 178

Unnecessary Electricity

I've been in the US for more than two and a half years. I love to stay here very much. But sometimes I feel a bit uncomfortable about the American lifestyle, because the American lifestyle is not ecological especially in power saving. American people seem to be unconcerned about power saving. They use a dryer for laundry, a dishwasher and a sprinkler and many homes are centrally heated. Actually, these are very convenient for us. But I think these things need much electricity. American people may use a lot of electricity every day and they may not care about it.

When I came to the US, I was surprised that there were not washing line poles in yards and verandahs. In Japan, we usually hang laundry out to dry. I wanted to dry washed clothes in the sun but I couldn't do that, because there was no place for it. So, I hang them to dry in a room at night. Hanging them to dry in a bedroom is a good humidifier and also I can save power. But I'm afraid that American people may be sorry for me to see hanging clothes to dry in a room, because I have heard that someone who does that is so poor that he/she can't afford to buy a dryer. Is it true?

Our family will go back to Japan this July, so some people have come to see our apartment. They turn on every light and a ventilating fan, but they never turn them off when they leave. My husband said the same thing before. His boss won't turn the light off when he goes home. So my husband turns it off almost every day. We are taught by parents and teachers that we have to turn lights off if we don't need them. I think American children are not told about power saving.

I don't say Japanese people have more environmental consciousness than Americans have. But the Japanese language has a word *mottainai*. Its meaning is "it's so wasteful when things are not made full use of their value." We are taught by our parents and teachers not to waste anything we have. Japanese, especially older people, don't like to waste things because we have a *mottainai* spirit. I've heard that English doesn't have an equivalent word to *mottainai*. I wonder if American people don't feel *mottainai* when they use unnecessary electricity. Simplicity and frugality are virtues in Japan. On the contrary, do simplicity and frugality feel like stinginess in America? I'm afraid that Japanese might forget the *mottainai* spirit, because Japanese people like to follow the American style.

Questions for Reflection:

1. Do most people in your home country dry their clothes with a power dryer, or by air? What about wash dishes? Heat their homes? Have you noticed any

other differences in resource use across cultures? What do you think fuels these differences?

2. Does your home language have a single word that means something like "it's so wasteful when things are not made full use of their value?

3. The author sees US Americans as wasteful. Do you agree or disagree? Why?

Comment: page 179

Valentine's Day

When one of my boys was born on Valentine's Day, many of my friends made a joke, "What a poor baby! He will always worry about how many chocolates he will get on his birthday." I used to reply to them, "It's OK, I will always prepare a big chocolate for him."

Yes, in Japan, Valentine's Day is so different from the western countries. In Japan, only the women give the gift of chocolate to men on that day. It is the big chance for shy women to show love to men. We have not only the real serious chocolate (Honmei Choco), but also the obligatory chocolate (Giri Choco). We prepare obligatory chocolates for almost every man who works together or has any relationship with us. For the women, this is a really exciting but annoying season, because we can prepare a wonderful special gift for a special person, but we also have to prepare many reasonable, equal chocolates for our co-workers.

If the men get a chocolate gift on Valentine's Day, they have to think about a return gift. In Japan, March 14th (White Day) is the day of returning the gift. If he loves that woman, he may return more expensive gifts or marshmallows. If he doesn't like her, he will prepare just cookies or candy. Is it a silly custom that the woman waits a whole month to see whether the man likes her or not?

Needless to say, Japanese Valentine's Day and White Day were made by Japanese sweet companies, but some Japanese people think these days are serious and count how many gifts they can get.

In the US, especially the younger grade classes have a Valentine's Day's card exchange. The teacher encourages the children to make a card for every classmate. The store sells candies with the cards and it is like another Halloween. My boys are excited to get the cards and don't care about which is the serious one and which is the obligatory one. Everybody can get the cards equally. The men prepare flowers or gifts for the women. We don't think about return gifts...How peaceful and thoughtful, Valentine's Day!

Questions for Reflection:

1. Is Valentine's Day celebrated in your home country? If so, what are the traditions? Does the expression of affection begin with women or with men? Why do you think this is?

2. In your home country, what holidays include some kind of obligation (to give a gift, to visit, to attend a service, to make a food)?

3. In your home country, what holidays involve different activities for men compared to women?

4. Which different cultural values are highlighted in the US vs. Japanese Valentine's Day described here?

Comment: page 180

Education

Are You Coming to My Conference, Dad? A Mother's View

Most Japanese mothers do not expect their husbands to go to their child's parent-teacher conference with them. In my case, I told my husband the date of the conference for my son in first grade. I asked him to go to the conference with me. Unfortunately, his answer was no, because he had a class to attend at his university around that time. I didn't ask him any more about the conference. Our conversation just stopped there. I naturally thought that it was my job to meet my son's teacher and listen to her and ask her about my son's progress at school, although I felt it was a little overwhelming for me.

I found myself quite surprised when I went to my son's school on the day of the conference. Wow! Parents, I mean both fathers and mothers, were coming together for their child's conference in all of the classrooms. I felt American parents were very eager to understand their child's education.

I was particularly impressed by the fathers who came to the conference, and immediately asked them some questions:

Q1: Is this your own choice to come to the conference?
A1: Yes, we both want to come together.
Q2: Why?
A2: (wife) Because we have different questions.
    (husband) Because my wife takes care of our children most of the time so I don't want her to be burdened. I think both fathers and mothers need to get involved in our children's education. I changed my work schedule and came to the conference today.

This father's words gave me a chance to reflect on Japanese fathers' involvement in education.

As my husband reacted in the beginning, most of the Japanese fathers tend not to change their work schedule to come to the conference, because their first priority is their business. Even though they may want to have time for their children, their companies don't allow them to have a chance to do so.

The concept of the Japanese company denies the fathers' role at home. If you make a mistake at your work in Japan, your boss might say you should go back home and just take care of your wife and children. Even today, our first priority is not the family. The family is considered as a place to support their business. Don't you think this is too old-fashioned?

Compared to Japanese society, thinking about the family seems to be the first priority in the US. There are many American fathers who are involved in their children's education and child-rearing on a daily basis around me. To me, they seem to be having a wonderful time with their children playing together and studying together.

In the US, I see some Japanese fathers who see their children off in the morning and pick them up at school in the afternoon. Actually, they are getting involved in their children's education here in the US more than in Japan. They are changing their attitude toward their children and starting to think that their involvement in education and child-rearing is so important for them.

By the way, what happened to my conference? Suddenly, my husband ran into the classroom in time and asked some questions about my son at school. That was so worthwhile for us. That night, my husband and son took a bath together, and they had a wonderful conversation about school.

Lastly, at the graduation ceremony at Harvard Business School, the dean gave a speech to the graduates. He said, "Think about your family first in your life."

I hope Japanese society allows us to get involved in more family events in the future. Isn't it an important thing to change your schedule and meet your precious children's teacher? I admire the American style of parenting.

Are You Coming to My Conference, Dad? A Father's Reply

In Japan, there is a day in the school year when parents visit their child's class to see what their child is doing in the classroom and how the class is going. It is a good chance for parents to see their child's attitude in the class and to have a chance to talk with the teacher. Mothers usually attend the class visit, however fathers don't. Maybe, Father is so busy with his work, maybe he doesn't think it is necessary, or Japanese society might not allow workers to have a day off for a school visit.

If we were staying in Japan, I might never have attended a school
conference for our children. The Japanese father says relatively little
to his child about education. We show our own attitude toward study
and work to our child, then the child can learn that from the father.
If you want to be a good chef of Japanese food and join in a famous
Japanese restaurant, nobody teaches you how to cook and nobody
suggests how to do seasoning. You have to look at how they are doing
it and find the seasoning from them by yourself.

Sometimes, the same things happen in companies in Japan. I think
it is one aspect of Japanese culture. When I was asked by my wife to
come to the school conference with her, my first answer was, "Why?"
I had never thought of attending a school conference with my wife,
because I thought my wife could take care of our children's education.

She told me that both fathers and mothers usually come to conferences and listen to teachers in the United States and we could ask the
teachers anything about education and school life. Both of us should
listen to what the teachers were doing and what the teachers thought
about our child and what we need for our child's future. We are staying in a foreign country which has a different culture from Japan. If
our children have any difficulties in their education or school life, we
have to help them to manage or overcome these, even if it seems no
problem at all when we are in Japan. When I found it necessary to
join the school conference, I agreed to come with my wife.

At my first school conference with the teachers, I was surprised to
find that every teacher had been looking at our child closely and
knew what our child could do and couldn't. There are many students
in a class, however, teachers are looking and thinking about each student very much. When I asked what our child needed to step up, they
advised us what was necessary and how to support our child. We had
a meaningful time with the teachers at the conference. That night,
I talked with my wife about the school conference. I told her that it
was great to know the status of our child in the class. We could share
an idea of education and future of our child.

Whenever I asked our children how they were in school, they just said "Good," but I couldn't see how good they were. I sometimes asked them what they did in the class today or what was interesting to them in the class, then they said a little bit more detail, but it was not enough to know a whole picture of their school life. After attending the school conference, I am able to see their school life more clearly than before. It is important to have a conference with teachers, because they make us have some ideas of their school life and give us some advice from the educational point of view. It is significant.

Next year, there was no question about attending the school conference together with my wife. We went to school and met a Japanese woman who had a conference with the teacher just before ours. She left the classroom alone. We said hello to her and talked a few words with each other, then said good-bye. After she walked away, I asked my wife, "Where is her husband?"

Questions for Reflection:

1. Did fathers attend school meetings and events when you were a child? Did your school have an individual parent-teacher conference about you?

2. What is the role of fathers vs. mothers in their children's education in your country? Do fathers and mothers ever volunteer to help in a classroom? Do they attend plays and sports events?

3. Think of a time you have adopted a new value or behavior of a new culture. What factors led to the change? How long had you been exposed to the new culture before the change occurred? Have you had the chance to return to your home country – and if so, how does this new value fit there?

4. Do you think it is easier to become a good chef if someone explains what seasonings to use, or is it better just to watch and experiment? Can children learn values just by watching and experimenting?

Comment: page 182

Being Absent from School

Traditionally, Koreans believe strongly that the duty of students is to study and that students should not miss school, where they can get a lot of knowledge. So, there are very few students who are absent from school. I missed school twice in 12 years, from elementary school to high school, but my sister and my elder brother were never absent from school for 12 years. They got 12-year All Attendance Prizes, which had been made to encourage not being absent from school. We believe perfect attendance at school symbolizes diligence and tolerance. Because of this belief, many Korean parents let children go to school even though they are a little sick so they will be trained to be strong through the experience of enduring sickness. And, if a child is absent from school, parents will be sorry for the teacher, as if their child hasn't done his duty.

When my family came here, I realized that Americans are not as concerned about being absent from school. One year ago my son, who had never been absent from school in Korea, told me with surprise that one of his classmates had missed classes for a long time and didn't know when he would come back from travel. And, I also heard that the school nurse had sent my friend's daughter home even though my friend had thought her daughter, who had been a little bit sick, could study at school.

It seems to me that Americans think about education flexibly and efficiently. They think traveling is also an education and is as important as studying at school because traveling makes children get real-life knowledge and develop emotion. They also think in order to get well fast, it is more efficient for children to rest at home than to be at school when they are sick. For a year and a half, I have been able to enjoy American flexibility and efficiency. My son missed class three times because of a trip and my daughter stayed at home many times because of sickness. Sometimes, I think the traditional ways of Korean education, like perfect attendance at school, were the best and quickest ways, at least in the past. They urged many able people who were diligent and good at studying to develop my country. However, I now think Korean education, which is making many children compete with each other in studying so much, should be changed to focus on making a person who is developed both intellectually and emotionally. In order to do that, the system of education needs to be flexible like that of America.

Even though I have this kind of thinking, I am still the one who tells my children automatically, "You should not be absent from school, although you are a little sick. You can endure." Or, "You missed class because of traveling. You better study in order to catch up with the class."

Questions for Reflection:

1. What is the typical school policy in your home country regarding school absences for sick children? For family travel? Is it OK to miss school if you are sick or taking a family trip?

2. Do children have an obligation to their teacher to be good students?

3. Can you think of an American value or custom that is quite different from what you are used to, and that you think is a good idea? Have you tried to adopt it? What happens when you try?

4. In Korea, "parents let children go to school even though they are a little sick so they will be trained to be strong through the experience of enduring sickness. And, if a child is absent from school, parents will be sorry for the teacher, as if their child hasn't done his duty." What are the advantages and/or disadvantages of this approach — for the child, the teacher, the other children in the class, and society?

Comment: page 184

Clean-Up Time

I have been wondering why American school students don't clean up their own classrooms, rest rooms, and stairs, etc. by themselves. I heard that they clean up their desks, but that's it.

In Japanese schools, every student has approximately 20 minutes of clean up time every afternoon. This clean up time is part of the school discipline. I think there are three main reasons for this.

The first reason is that everybody should do their own things by themselves. It is natural for us to clean up our own mess.

The next reason is that the students learn the importance of cooperation through cleaning up. Usually they are separated into groups of five to six by lottery or something. If all the members don't cooperate, they will not finish their work within the clean- up time, so they devise effective ways of cleaning up. This could be one of the good opportunities for them to communicate with each other.

The final reason is that they can learn a common way to do clean up time. For example, when they clean up their classrooms, at first they have to move their desks to one corner of the room. Then some of them sweep the floor with small brooms and others wipe the floor with mops or floor cloths, because Japanese school floors are mostly made of tile. Then they put the desks back to the right places. Last, they sweep and wipe the corner where they had placed the desks.

This process is sometimes hard work for young children. Some students may not like clean up time. But many of them would realize the importance of keeping their rooms clean. They would not want to make a mess, because they know the difficulty of cleaning up. Probably they won't scribble or throw away trash where there is no trash can. They will come to thank those who clean up the public places or their homes.

I admire the American style education in many ways, but when I see the mess in the school, I am a little bit disappointed. How do you feel about it?

Questions for Reflection:

1) What do the clean-up practices described here reveal about the author's culture? What are the clean-up expectations for children in your culture? What cultural values do these expectations reveal?

2) Have you ever had to adjust to different classroom or workplace social norms or expectations? What were they and what was that experience like?

3) What value lesson do you think American children learn from having a school janitor clean their classroom? The author makes a compelling case for the value of having children clean their own classrooms. What are the positive and negative aspects to the US system and the Japanese system described here?

Comment: page 185

Examination Hell in Japan

In Japan we have an examination for entering famous national and private kindergartens and elementary schools. These schools are attached to a high school and university. We are attracted to these schools because children who go there have a very good chance of going to the best schools and universities. Parents who believe it is a good choice for their child wish to enroll their child in these schools. My first child experienced such an entrance examination. He studied for 2 hours every day when he was only 3 years old. He was admitted and went to a private kindergarten and elementary school till second grade in Japan. We were relieved about this course.

We have many supplementary private schools to prepare children for examinations. If the parents decide the child should take an examination, the child goes there and studies. At examinations for kindergarten and elementary school, the student alone and then the parent and child together undergo an oral examination. Then the child's common sense ability, creative power and physical strength are tested. For junior high school and above, all subjects are tested by a written examination.

Although taking such an examination for kindergarten is not so common, many Japanese children begin to study seriously for an examination for entering junior high school when they are in third grade. After school they have a supplementary lesson from 3:00 to 5:00 in their school. Then, they take private lessons from 5:30 to 11:00pm every day. They have no time for play dates with their friends.

Fortunately we have had a chance to live in America. We could have a change from the Japanese way of thinking. My children are having a good time and a valuable experience now. They are excited for play dates and sports every day. My sons have joined a soccer team and have taken up golf, baseball, and tennis. It is better than we had hoped for American life. We feel able to climb up from examination hell!!!

Questions for Reflection:

1. What do you think about a system of young children studying hard in order to gain entrance to a school that promises to lead them to a good future? Is this expectation common in your native culture? What are the advantages and disadvantages of this system, and what cultural values does it reveal?

2. What do you think of young children spending their free time playing games and doing sports? Is this expectation/practice common in your native culture? What are the advantages and disadvantages of a system that promotes play and sports? What cultural values are revealed by this practice?

3. The author shifted between the cultural norms of Japanese and US cultures, depending on the context. Have you ever shifted between different sets of

cultural norms? What was that experience like? How long had you been in
your host culture before this shift?

4. Have you ever had the experience of returning to your home country after having adapted/adhered to some cultural norms/values from your host country?
   What did that experience feel like? If you have not lived abroad, think of a
   time when you have had to adjust to new cultural norms (i.e. going from high
   school to college or switching jobs/companies). What was that experience
   like? Is there anything you could have done to better prepare yourself for that
   experience?

Comment: page 186

Learning Math and How to Think

When I help my son to do his homework, I often feel the difference in
how children learn math in America and Japan.

In Japan, we have textbooks which are used at school. Of course there
are a few companies for school textbooks, but the content is almost
the same. Children learn math along with the textbook, including
learning how to calculate. After children understand how to calculate, they practice the calculation a lot. In the second grade children
need to memorize the multiplication table from one to nine. In many
schools, teachers check the time children need to say the multiplication table from one to nine so that they can memorize it perfectly.
That is why many Japanese are good at calculation in their head.

I found an interesting difference in learning multiplication at American schools. When my children learn how to calculate multiplication
here, they have been taught to draw horizontal lines and vertical
lines. For example, when they calculate 3x4, they draw three horizontal lines and then draw four vertical lines on them, and they count
the number of intersections. I have never known how to think like
that.

In an American school, it is most important for children to learn how to think. My sons have a textbook for math but they never bring it back home, so I actually don't know how they are learning math. I just see their printed homework, and they are often required to explain how to think. When we had just moved here, it was hard for us to explain our thinking with our limited English. But now my oldest son says math in America is like a quiz and interesting, but in Japan it is just practicing calculation and is boring.

"How do you think?" This is always required in America not only in learning math.

In Japan we are often required to cooperate with others, and we are not good at explaining our original thinking, because we haven't been trained to do this. So it is hard to raise persons who have leadership in Japan. I hope that my sons learn how to think about various things while we are here.

Questions for Reflection:

1. Did you have textbooks, drills, and practice worksheets when you were learning math in primary school? Were you encouraged to think critically about math as a child or was the emphasis on learning "facts"? What about other subjects — history, or science, for example? Which teaching style do you think works best? Why? Does your answer depend on a child's age or the academic subject? What do your responses to these questions reveal about your own cultural values?

2. Should teachers be concerned about whether their students enjoy school? Why or why not?

3. The author points out that in her culture all students, regardless of what school they go to, use textbooks with the same content and are taught through rote memorization, while children in the US are taught using various approaches and types of textbooks. How does each educational model reflect its respective culture? What are the strengths and benefits of each model?

Comment: page 187

Make-up, Hair styles and Clothes of Teenage Girls

It is common for girls to be interested in dressing fashionably. And it is very difficult to control that. When I was a junior high school student, the school regulations about our outward appearance were very strict. Regarding hairstyles, for instance, bangs had to be cut above the eyebrow. In other words, bangs below the eyebrow were bad (wrong). Although in high school there was no such regulation, we were forbidden to get a permanent in our hair. Make-up was prohibited. Even lipstick and pierced ears were not allowed. Moreover, teachers inspected their students suddenly, and punished those who broke their regulation.

Maybe nowadays, it is not so strict. But school uniforms, called *seifuku* remain in almost every school (except the international school and a few private schools). The typical style of *seifuku* is a white blouse and dark blue or black skirt (and a jacket in winter). The length of skirt is regulated. Sometimes, the teacher measures that. We can't wear different styles of course. Besides the skirt, the color of socks, the length of socks and how to tie the ribbon on the blouse are also regulated.

As a matter of course, the students rebel. Some students pretend to be a good student in front of the teacher, and transform themselves just as they leave the school. On the other hand, I heard that many girls are choosing their high school by its uniform recently. Some schools have a famous fashion designer design their school uniforms, because it is good for their business. So girls attain more "cute" and "stylish" school uniforms. I think this is shameful, and is the result of excessive, meaningless regulations.

Also in Japan, many teenage girls are influenced in their clothes and make-up by TV stars. Last year, terrible thick-soled dangerous sandals were in fashion. And as for make-up, recently some girls prefer to make up weird. There are so many fashion magazines for teenagers in Japan, girls can get information easily. And they copy that. After all, Japanese teenage girls are bound by regulations in school. On the other hand, they are enjoying their fashion after school.

In America students seem to be free in choosing their clothes for school. When I went to our local public high school during the daytime, I was surprised that their styles were varied. And I was particularly shocked at the girls who wore tank tops like lingerie. They look like the adults they can see in fashion magazines. I think individuality is valuable, but in school, students should wear clothes suitable for study.

Questions for Reflection:

1. Did you wear clothes that were "suitable for studying" when you were in high school? Did your parents' idea of "suitable" and your idea of "suitable" differ? Where you are from, what do teenagers wear to school now? Are there rules about dressing that they must follow? What does this say about cultural norms/values?

2. Which is more important to most people in your culture: helping young people express their individuality or helping young people concentrate on their studies? Why do think that is? What rules, if any, do you think are appropriate for what teenagers should wear to school?

3. Is it a good thing or a bad thing for all teenagers in a school to be dressed alike? Why? What does this teach?

Comment: page 188

Parent Involvement

In Japan parents have fewer opportunities to go to their children's school than in the US. This is because most Japanese children go to and from school by themselves. And parents are not asked to come to the classroom to help with special projects or to go with children on school trips. We usually entrust only the teacher with education in school.

We would think it is unfair for a parent with a special skill to help only one class. Also, our society believes that teachers are professionals and should not be interrupted by parents. Of course, American teachers are professionals, too. But perhaps the situation is similar to doctors in an operating room – parents are not invited there in either country. We think that going into the classroom is a little bit like going into the operating room – we should leave it to the professionals and not go there.

In a sense, it is very comfortable for parents to send children to school. Parents can have more free time for themselves, so some mothers can get jobs after their children enter elementary school. (The income, however, is sometimes set aside for children's educational expenses.)

Though we have fewer opportunities to join our children's class in Japan, every school has a Parent Teacher Association. Most parents are involved in PTA activities. The PTA does a variety of things on Saturdays, Sundays, or in the evening. For example, they have meetings to discuss school problems and student's issues. They collect waste articles for school fund raising. They put good books in the school library. They plant flowers in the school garden or dig weeds for making a good educational environment.

There are several ways Japanese parents are involved in schools that I have not seen in the US: (1) Japanese schools hold an observation day several times a year. Then we can observe our children's class. (At these times, the teacher and children are nervous, so perhaps the atmosphere in the class is a little bit different from usual.) (2) The teacher usually visits every child's home once a year. The teacher observes the children's rooms and their playing places. It helps the teachers understand the children's circumstances. (3) We have an athletic meet once a year. It's very fun. Of course most events are taken part in by children, but there are some that we parents can join. We enjoy the baton relay and tug of war with the children.

Thus in many cases, Japanese parents are involved in schools indirectly. In contrast, in the US, parents have comparatively more opportunities to join their children's class.

Questions for Reflection:

1. How much variety in teaching methods from teacher to teacher is there in your home country? Do most teachers teach using the same curricular materials, or is there a big range? What does this reveal about your culture's shared values?

2. Do parents help out in schools in your home country? Do they volunteer to help children learn to read, take the class to trips to their workplace, or share other special talents? What does this system illustrate about your culture?

3. Which do you think is more important — that every child in a culture have a very similar experience that is as good as possible, or that every teacher have the encouragement to offer the best learning experience possible, even if children's experiences are quite different? What are the advantages of these two approaches? The disadvantages?

Comment: page 190

Parent Involvement, Grades and Modesty in School

I found a lot of differences with my children related to their school here. I would like to share several of my feelings.

First, in Japan, we think school and teachers are the authority. We think school is a kind of sacred place that the parents can't be involved in. We believe the school is perfect and don't say negative things to the teachers. But in America, we have a lot of chance to be involved in the curriculum. We can send a letter to the teacher, principal or even superintendent if we feel unsatisfied. We have many volunteer opportunities in the school. I think the American system is more open than those in Asian countries. I'm really glad that we can be involved in the children's education. On the other hand, we think we should respect the teachers, so we hesitate to call teachers by their first name. I'm wondering if the teachers feel I am being too polite when I address them with an honorific title after they address me with my first name. But if I use the first name to address teachers, I'm embarrassed that the teacher may think I am so rude.

Second, we take report card scores more seriously. I always fight with my son because I always ask him to get higher points. If my son gets 95%, I ask him, "Why did you miss 5%?" and encourage him to earn 100%. But in America, if children get 75%, parents cheer their efforts. We think good achievement is a family honor and failure is a family shame. So many Asian kids have a lot of pressure before tests. American teachers say they don't understand this pressure, because they think the test results are only one day's score, so children may have a bad day or a good day. But we think the children should prepare for the test anytime.

The conference is the same way. In America, the teacher says only the good points and just a little bit about bad points. As an Asian parent, we always would like to see more plan for improvement, so we would like to listen to the bad point first.

We don't have a reward for natural behavior, but in America, they prepare such rewards. For example, many classrooms have a marble jar and if kids did a great job or had a great attitude, they can put a marble in there and if it is filled up, they can have a party! I sometimes think the American style spoils children. I agree that we should admire their effort, but still think if they have a little bit of pressure, they can make better results. My children have already gotten used to the American style, so if I speak more strictly with much pressure, they feel discouraged.

Third, we think modesty is a virtue. We believe harmony is more necessary than uniqueness. During a discussion, we keep quiet and always observe the surrounding appearance. But in America, we can't hesitate to show our opinion. Children are encouraged to say anything and American students don't fear making mistakes. Again, American teachers praise the children even if they speak very wrongly. I think we should learn this American style to show our opinion to anybody, because it makes the children establish self-confidence, but still I am wondering when American children learn to wait and think more before they speak up.

Those differences between America and Japan are on my mind. Since we have lived here for 7 years, my children love only the American style, but I want them to learn both (American and Japanese) good styles.

Questions for Reflection:

1. Are schools in your home country more similar to how Japan is described here, or to the US?

2. Which style do you prefer— having an open and egalitarian relationship with a teacher, or having a lot of deference and respect for a teacher? Why? Does

your answer depend on the age of the child?

3. Do you learn better when an instructor starts by pointing out your mistakes or starts by pointing out what you have done right? Why?

4. Which is more important to you – to be able to express opinions clearly and confidently, or to be able to maintain harmonious relationships with people even if that means not expressing your real views? Why?

5. Have you had the experience of being caught between two sets of cultural values? What was that experience like? What did you learn from the experience?

6. Do you and your family, colleagues, or friends ever disagree about which system or cultural value is better?

Comment: page 191

School Lunch

The school lunch in Japan has very important educational roles besides being a time for consuming food. Students are expected to learn many values through their school lunch.

Students prepare lunch by themselves, starting in first grade. The students in charge wear white aprons, white caps and masks. They carry very heavy containers from the school kitchen to the classroom. Then they serve food to their classmates. Before eating, the students say in unison, *itadakimasu.* At the end of the meal, they say, *gochiso samadeshita.* These are words of appreciation for those who prepared the food. In all these ways, students are supposed to learn cooperation, responsibility and independence from adults.

School lunches in Japan are nutritionally well balanced. Milk, bread or rice, stew with meat and vegetable, and fruits. This is the typical menu. There are more than one hundred kinds of food for school lunch in a year. Menus are not repeated within the same month. They generally taste good. Most students look forward to lunch time. Mothers really trust it, too. Even if children don't eat much breakfast or dinner, as long as they eat the school lunch, we feel they get enough nutrition.

Students have lunch in their own home rooms with their home room teachers. All students in a school (and in some cases, all students in a town) eat the same lunch. There is no choice. Students, especially those in higher grades, are expected to finish the lunch unless they are allergic to something. Teachers supervise students not to leave their lunch uneaten.

I was so surprised that students at my child's school in the US stay at the cafeteria unsupervised by their home room teachers. It also surprised me that they throw away food, even food that is wrapped and could easily be saved. Japanese have the value that food is very precious so we must not waste it. Parents and teachers have taught children that value repeatedly.

Japanese mothers basically support the school lunch program, including the rule that children must finish their food. However it makes some students feel uncomfortable. I remember that one boy who hated tomatoes and couldn't eat them got punished by his teacher. He made him put the tomato on his desk and gaze at it the rest of the day.

We are concerned that the rule of completing the school lunch is so strict that it could be a burden for some children. However, we Japanese mothers accept its educational meaning. Generally, the evaluation of Japanese school lunch is very high.

Questions for Reflection:

1. When you were a school child, where did you eat lunch? Is the system the same for today's children? How does it compare to what the author describes

in Japan and the US? What cultural values do children in your home country learn from their school lunch period?

2. In your culture, do most people think children should have choices about what they eat, whom they play with, or what activity to engage in? How do you think this compares to other cultures?

3. What are the advantages of the school lunch system in Japan, as described here? What are the advantages of the school lunch system in the US? Disadvantages of each? What do these systems teach us about each respective culture? What would each culture have to give up if it tried to be more like the other country? What might each gain?

4. Choice is very important to many Americans, who generally don't like being told what to do or what to eat by the government. Can you think of other examples of Americans resisting government control, or valuing choice?

Comment: page 193

Self-Confidence

My first impression of the US was that most American people speak so confidently. While I was watching the news on TV, many ordinary people who were asked questions by the newscaster could answer the questions so confidently. They were not experts but didn't hesitate to answer the questions. I have been wondering where such self-confidence comes from. Most Japanese people are not accustomed to speaking or performing in front of a large audience, except for a few people such as politicians, presidents of companies, or teachers.

Because our society is so homogeneous in many ways, we can understand each other easily. And our traditional virtue is to be modest. We have been taught to be modest and cooperate with other people. Especially after World War II, our education system emphasized equality. In our school schedule, we rarely had individual performance time; rather, we did everything as a group. (Recently the system has been changing.) So Japanese children do not learn very much about how to speak confidently or persuade others.

On the contrary, American society is very diverse in many ways. You can't be modest. When you want to be understood by others, you have to have a strong opinion and convince others effectively. To speak confidently is very important to live in this society.

And I found why American people could speak so confidently. It is in the education system. When my children entered their schools, they had to do Sharing once a week in front of their classmates. After Sharing they got a big round of applause, and their self-confidence grew. From such early days, American people have practiced speaking up or performing in front of audiences. They are not hesitant to speak. And I really admire the American high school debate classes because many students who take the class can improve their speaking skills. In today's world, we need such abilities to persuade others or negotiate for something with others. I think we should adopt American active and positive attitudes.

Questions for Reflection:

1. Did you have such a Sharing or "Show and Tell" opportunity in school when you were a child?

2. Do you think that telling your opinion to a newscaster is an immodest thing to do? Would you feel comfortable doing it?

3. Can a person be both modest and self-confident? How does your culture teach children its values about modesty? About self-confidence?

4. Compare the US and another country in terms of modesty – how much is modesty valued? Who is expected to be modest – both men and women? Young and old people? Educated and non-educated people? What happens when someone is not modest?

5. Compare the US and another country in terms of self-confidence – how much is it valued? Who is expected to be self-confident – just professionals and

experts, or everybody? Children?

6. The author connects the homogeneity of Japanese society with the virtue of modesty. How might these two be related to each other?

Comment: page 194

Some Educational Philosophy Differences

Since I moved to the US less than three months ago, I cannot tell all the differences between the US and Taiwan in detail. Nevertheless, there were some themes I would like to propose for discussion. Through the situation of my child's performance, volunteering for the school's math games activity, and attending the conference to discuss with my daughter's teacher, I found some differences of teaching philosophy between these two countries.

First, students in the US are asked younger than in Taiwan to actively engage in thought-provoking activity that involves looking at a critical issue and the dilemma of social study. Their contribution to class discussions will be evaluated as part of their academic record. This aim of teaching urges students to learn more thoughtfully and more meaningfully about what really happened and to develop the ability to make inferences. However, too many of these thoughtful discussion activities can cause less focusing on the main theme and can reduce the time and effort spent on drilling until the new knowledge can be applied automatically.

Second, because the number of students in a classroom in the US is only about half the number in Taiwan, teachers show more willingness to encourage students to raise their hand to seek the teacher's assistance at any time. Students learn how to ask for help and some-

times learn the skills of problem solving. Quickly solving learning difficulties often reduces the struggle and helpless feelings, especially
for those students who come from another country. For example,
my daughter cannot speak English well, so her teacher asks her to
raise her hand any time she has a problem. Although she cannot
speak well, she can listen well. She knows what her teacher is saying most of the time. Whenever she has a problem her teacher has
sensed it before she raised her hand. Her teacher kept on requesting
us to encourage her to ask questions more often. She also managed
some chances for her to cooperate with her classmates to solve math
problems together. I think it would be hard for teachers to notice
every student's individual need if they have more than 35 students
to take care of at the same time. Teachers in Taiwan have to do some
adjustment to extend the best outcome of teaching and learning; they
would allow three to five questions at the discussion time and would
often end in a hurry.

Third, students in the US do not have formal textbooks for most subjects and they drill and practice new words without a relevant essay
or article to help them rehearse to make those words meaningful.
Parents in Taiwan catch on to what their children might have learned
in school by browsing the textbooks.

The list above can only be mentioned as my personal view. I don't
intend to imply which philosophy of education is better because each
education system has been suitably formed circumstantially to the
value and culture where it belonged. In Taiwan, most teachers would
follow the standard curriculum to fulfill the teaching objectives set
by the Ministry of Education. Consequently, it would be easy for
them to predict the level of a newcomer student's prior knowledge
base. Some of my friends in the US have found that the materials and
courses provided by the teachers at the same grade were somewhat
different; therefore it might have produced some variation between
students. When I was an elementary school teacher I was a member
of my school's curriculum development committee. We used to meet
two weeks before the first school day of a school year to review all

teaching materials and the teaching plan to make sure that all the teaching goals between grades remained consistent and systematic.

My daughter has changed a lot after she came to the US. She has more time to do some arts and crafts and to enjoy outdoor activities. She asks questions more often. She even told me that she would like to stay here longer because she has less homework to do than in Taiwan. It always took her more than two hours to finish her math and language homework everyday including weekends. Now she doesn't have to do homework daily and the homework is easy except in social studies. This means she has lots of leisure time for playing, reading and exploring. Education is a life long matter; it is hard to tell which system is superior within a short period of time.

Questions for Reflection:

1. Did you have textbooks, drills, and practice worksheets when you were a young student? Were you encouraged to think critically about social issues as a child? Which teaching style do you think works best? Why? Does your answer depend on a child's age or the academic subject?

2. When you were a student, did the teacher encourage you to ask for individual help? If not, what did you do if you did not understand something?

3. How much should teachers try to ensure that their students enjoy school?

4. What are the advantages to a society of all children learning from the same curriculum and textbooks? What are the advantages to a society of teachers making their own choices about curriculum, teaching methods, and materials?

5. Have you had the experience of seeing something done very differently in two different cultural, sub-cultural, or organizational contexts and not being sure which way you think is best?

Comment: page 195

Textbooks

Every April when I was a student, looking at the cherry blossoms out of the classroom window, I used to feel my fluttering heart as brand-new textbooks were supplied by the school into my hands. It is a very common scene on the first day of a new term in Japanese schools. In Japan, the government requires the use of textbooks that have been specified by educational guidelines. Teachers can choose from six types of textbooks, all of which have been approved by the national government, because our educational system puts a value on teaching equally to all students. There is a very little room for a teacher's originality.

When my daughter was in her first day of a new semester here in Lawrence School, she did not get any textbooks at all. Several days later, I realized that students were not provided their own textbooks in grades K 2. They learn some subjects using worksheets that each class teacher may choose, indicating that the U.S. teachers can use their personal preference. It is unique that the U.S. educational system leaves so many choices to the teacher, town, and state, suggesting it must have a great diversity in terms of focus, style, and quality. Japanese textbooks are thin and light so students can take them home to do homework every day. Students can write notes or underline in their own textbooks. We believe knowledge is needed as a means to realize the purpose of education, which is to extract human potential. We think memorized knowledge is valuable. Our exam system is severely strict and a heavy load on students. This helps the knowledge level to some extent.

American textbooks are thick and heavy because they have a lot of details with color photographs or illustrations. Students are expected to express themselves, and these details help them do so. Students who express themselves are valued because the schools value each student's personality and originality. Students have to leave their textbooks in their school because they are a part of the public equipment.

In short, both systems seem to take an extreme position. We might be producing ready-made people. America might tend to produce free-thinking people. Freedom of expression and self-assertion are totally different, but we confuse them easily. We have to produce people with high hopes, since it is they who will be building our future.

Comment: page 196

Writing Letters Neatly

Recently, I realized one of my boy's writing was so rough. He can't hold the pencil the right way, therefore he can't write the letters neatly. His letters are curved and the size is different.

In Japan, we have the subject *kakikata* (penmanship/calligraphy) at least once a week. In the first grade, we learn the exact correct posture (back should be straight, we need one rock hand between desk and stomach, the feet should be on the floor), how to hold the pencil, how to put the other hand on the paper. Children in the younger grades start by using a pencil and gradually it changes to a marker and calligraphy brush. During this subject, we also learn how to write letters neatly; an upward or downward brush stroke, stopping etc. are very important to show the beautiful way. Through the class, the student's writing will improve without realizing it. Some strict teachers often make the student rewrite the letter if the student doesn't write it neatly and accurately. Japanese has three types of characters (*Hiragana, Katakana* and *Kanji*) and their origins were related to each other. Some letters are similar. Therefore it is important to write the letters neatly and practice them. There are a lot of calligraphy classes and competitions. It is popular for younger children to go to a calligraphy class. (Older kids are busy going to cram school.) Some Japanese pencil companies also provide an instrument that helps children hold the pencil with the right angle and exact way. They also make triangle pencils, which fit easily into the hands of younger children and they can learn how to hold the pencil correctly. In this way, Japanese people really think the neat writing is important.

Here, English has only 26 alphabets letters. My children said there sometimes is a class about how to write the alphabet in order or copy the letters neatly. To my surprise, the stroke order is different from the books. The teacher's sheet sometimes suggests practicing the letters with open eyes and closed eyes. (I believe it is just for fun…) And the teacher always praises my son's rough letters.
If I really try to fix my son's handwriting, I will have to do it by myself. I asked my parents to send those useful kits or some textbooks from Japan. I hope it will work for my children

Questions for Reflection:

1. How much emphasis was put on proper handwriting when you were a child in school? How much is put on it now, relative to typing/keyboarding?

2. Do people in your home country have distinctive handwriting styles? That is, can you tell whether something was written by your mother vs. friend vs. brother? What does the teaching/encouragement (or not) of distinctive writing styles tell us about cultural values?

3. When you see writing that is "messy" (e.g., uneven in shape and size), what, if anything, do you conclude about the writer? Why?

4. Do you think it is more important for a teacher to help a child practice a skill over and over so that he/she completes it with perfection, or to help a child get "good enough" at a skill that he/she can use it to other things? Why? What does your answer reveal about your own cultural values?

Comment: page 198

Comments

Communication

American Courtesy
Hyeryoung Jung
Korea

Please read descriptions of:

Interpersonal Boundaries
Value Changes
Modesty
Communication Style

Comment:

Hyeryoung originally wrote this story as a description of two un-related things she had noticed about the US – (a) friendliness and politeness and (b) how teachers use words of encouragement in schools. But they are both similarly focused on the implicit expecta-tions we have about the expression of emotions between people. Hyeryoung is surprised that Americans choose to pierce the bubble of anonymity she is used to, by speaking to strangers in the store or on the street. Children share goody bags and write notes of appreciation. Teachers say "great!" at the drop of a hat, in the belief that those who feel good about their abilities will learn more easily. Thanks, chats and enthusiasm bubble up, directly and in words, everywhere, or so it feels to Hyeryoung. In fact, she chooses the word "stingy" to describe herself (an interesting cultural-value shift in itself).

Stories on a similar theme:

I Recommend Your Children Do Sports in America (Communication)
My Struggle with Discipline and Praise (Communication)

Apologies
Noriko Watanabe
Japan

Please read descriptions of:

Burdening Others
Value Changes
Modesty

Comment:

One of the most interesting aspects of cultural study is the way languages bundle emotions differently into little word packets. Everyone can recognize that feeling of "gosh, thank you, I'm sorry you had to go to that trouble, but I do appreciate it." But English-speakers don't have a single word – like *sumimasen* – for that complex emotion.

Other languages offer other examples. To translate *gemütlich* from German we need a string of words — cozy, comfortable, warm, pleasant. Edith Wharton, in her book *French Ways and Their Meaning,* takes eight pages to explain how the English word "love" differs from the French *l'amour.* (In brief, "love" is pure and poetic and

124

presumably life-long; *l'amour* has the same sense of poetry with a dash of romance and sensuality.) The Polish word *tesknota* is loosely translated as "nostalgia" but in Polish there is a larger dose of sadness and longing than in English. English speakers know these emotions – appreciation with gratitude, warm coziness, love with romance, and sad nostalgia. But the English language suggests that these emotions are not as central to our experience.

The other issue raised in this story is the nature of apology. Many cultural values are reflected in that moment when we decide whether or not to say, "I'm sorry." How important is it "not to make friction and to smooth over relationships?" Smooth relationships are desirable everywhere, of course. But so are other values – wanting to be recognized for one's individual accomplishments, wanting not to be unfairly blamed, wanting to "explore and act" more than to "be in relation to others," to name a few. Cultures (and individual people) differ in how they rank the importance of these.

In the individualistic US, "having a smooth relationship" sometimes sags in the ranking. The words "I'm sorry" seem to be absent in the Customer Service vocabulary, for example. A little smoothing could go a long way, but as Noriko notes, in English, an apology often connotes acceptance of blame and then becomes a complex act with potential legal consequences.

Stories on a similar theme:

I'm Sorry (Communication)
The Reason Why We Are Silent (Communication)

Body Distance
Noriko Watanabe
Japan

Please read descriptions of:
Individualism and Collectivism
Culture Shock Cycle
Communication Style

Comment:

Personal distance – the amount of space we prefer to have between us and another person – is highly dependent on many factors: how we are feeling at the moment, how well we know the other person, what activity we are doing, and … culture. If we do not understand this cultural aspect, it is very easy to mis-attribute unfamiliar personal distance to some personality or character trait. The person who stands just a few inches "too far away" (but just the right distance in her own culture) seems distant and aloof. Standing "too close" may feel aggressive or flirtatious, and actually hugging can feel inappropriately intimate.

Then, to make things even more complicated, we add in a psychological piece to the physical one. In a crowded place like a Japanese train where touching strangers is unavoidable, a kind of psychological bubble of privacy takes effect, and the touching is simply ignored. In a large, relatively less crowded country like the US, we have not developed such a psychological privacy bubble; intrusions into personal physical space must be apologized for. Kiss a friend but don't bump a stranger.

Noriko also points out some other ways that human connection and intimacy can be communicated, counterbalancing any lack of public hugging. Researchers have found Japanese parents to have more "skin to skin" contact with their young children (like in the bath tub) and, in general, to promote a kind of dependence when American parents are promoting independence. From these early child-rearing moments come many deeply rooted cultural differences.

Noriko points out that in Japan, sleeping in the same room as one's child is a common way for parents to bond with their children. In the US, parents are usually encouraged to sleep away from their babies. In fact, many pediatricians in the US encourage parents not to sleep in the same room with their infants, and not to pick up their babies every time they cry, so that they learn how to self-soothe.

These differences between Japanese and US parent/child child-rearing and sleeping patterns also echo the deeply- rooted value placed on individualism vs. collectivism in each culture. Many Americans begin to promote their children's independence in infancy by teaching them to sleep alone, while Noriko describes a Japanese custom of bathing and sleeping together throughout childhood. (In fact, parents and children may bathe together even as adults in Japan, allowing a time for personal and intimate conversation – a rare occurrence in the US, indeed, one that would raise eyebrows.) How cultures balance the demands for connection and independence is a complex one, one that is highlighted in this story.

Finally, note Noriko's earnest desire to correct any misinterpretation of the Japanese norms about physical contact. She knows how wrong it would be to think of Japanese mothers as cold or uncaring, and wants to describe the joy of closeness they experience in different ways. Being misperceived is one of the hardest aspects of being an expatriate.

Stories on a similar theme:

Greeting (Communication)
How to React to Compliments (Communication)
The Bow (Communication)

The Bow
Eun Young Lee
Korea

Please read descriptions of:

Power Distance

Comment:

Perhaps there is no simple act that sets the stage for a cultural encounter more clearly than the way we greet each other. Eun Young describes how a bow is used in Korea as a way to show respect to elders and for important, solemn occasions, but also – done differently, not so low, eyes down, the head just so – as a simple gesture of humility. In cultures where hierarchical relationships – boss/employee; elder/younger; teacher/student; parent/child – form an important axis of social interactions, the child is expected to master this non-verbal communication device. The display of humility, modesty and respect is a comfortable and important part of interpersonal relationships.

But in cultures where egalitarianism is an ideal (even if an un-realized one), bowing rings of subservience or servitude and is rarely seen except by performers receiving applause – unless one has occasion to meet a king. In these cultures, bowing almost evokes a visceral repulsion, touching a deep nerve connected to the belief that social status differences should be minimized. Children in the mainstream of these cultures are taught that looking someone "in the eye" is a way to show respect, honesty, and openness – and conversely, "avoiding" eye contact suggests sneakiness or guilt. No wonder so much cultural mis-communication occurs around this simple gesture!

Stories on a similar theme:

Body Distance (Communication)
Greeting (Communication)
The Reason Why We Are Silent (Communication)

English and Japanese Language
Tomoko Shimitzu
Japan

Please read descriptions of:

Communication Style
High vs. Low Context
Harmony and Face

Comment:

In this story, Tomoko shares an experience that illuminates key differences between communication styles, as well as the challenges inherent in using a communication style that is not appropriate in one's native culture. Tomoko notes a preference among Japanese to speak in an indirect and circular fashion is the norm. She is also describing an inductive style – the arguments are offered first, with the conclusion at the end. This communication style promotes values that are central to Japanese culture, such as harmony, face, and collectivism.

In contrast, Americans tend to use a deductive style – the main point is offered first, followed by supporting arguments. (In elementary school, for example, they may be taught to write an introductory paragraph that states their main thesis, then go on to support that thesis. This same format is the preferred one in academic writing throughout the education system, and in newspapers and public speeches as well.) In the US, people have a preference for a more direct, linear communication style, which is clearly captured in the American expression, "Say what you mean and mean what you say." When someone doesn't "get to the point" quickly, impatience on the part of the listener often ensues.

In Tomoko's case, communicating in a linear, direct and deductive way would not only sound abrupt, aggressive and rude to another Japanese person, but would also challenge her core cultural values and identity as a Japanese woman. It's no wonder that speaking in this way feels aggressive to Tomoko!

Formality and Informality
Sam-Sung Ko
Korea

Please read descriptions of:
Power Distance
Formality and Informality

Comment:

Sam-Sung points out some key cultural differences between her home culture and US culture. Her observation of the low-power distance situation she encountered in the US paints a clear picture of how confusing intercultural transition can be, especially when many of the basic "rules" of behavior are different than what we expect. Her higher power distance background led her to expect a formal speech, impersonal introductions, and a tone of solemnity, marks of a status differential between the new staff members and the Dean and faculty. For her, this underscoring of a status difference is comfortable and, indeed, efficient.

Instead, she encountered an entirely different approach in the US, where informality and low-power distance behavior are the norm. The US dean and professors offered a low power distance "gift" of personal access, and an opportunity to get to be known as an individual. The expectation of "schmoozing" with people on all levels of the social or professional hierarchy, or approaching authority figures directly, and often by their first names, can feel uncomfortable to those who have been taught to maintain a degree of formality and to show respect through deference. The task can feel even more daunting in a new language, with new rules. It is no wonder that Sam-Sung was taken aback by these cultural differences.

Sam-Sung also points out some of the advantages and disadvantages of both sets of cultural values. Her ability to analyze and acknowledge the validity of both approaches is a clear sign that she is well into the acculturation process.

Greeting
Hye Young Yoon
Korea

Please read descriptions of:

Power Distance
Value Changes
Individualism and Collectivism

Comment:

Hye Young was chagrined when she realized she had ignored the dental professor's outstretched hand. That experience of realizing that we have done the "wrong thing" is surely familiar to anyone who has traveled or moved to a new country. She appreciates that the professor would [surely] use his experience in Korea to interpret her behavior accurately.

She describes in vivid detail how uncomfortable she is with shaking hands with this older, esteemed man. Such deeply-felt emotions go along with these simple greeting rituals. For her, everything that she has been taught about how to behave at her husband's school interview can be signaled in an appropriate bow – to show respect, be humble, be polite, be a good guest. These are all the right attitudes to convey in a high power distance culture.

The act of shaking hands would, for her, feel void of any meaning and it feels awkward and limp, and perhaps especially awkward for a younger woman. In contrast, for a low-power-distance American, the act of shaking hands – and making eye contact at the same time – conveys similarly deeply-felt emotions, but different ones. It shows eagerness, confidence, and openness. What a different list! No wonder the experience stayed with Hye Young for a long time.

Hye Young also notes several other differences in greeting customs – whether to acknowledge strangers or not, and whether to display emotions (positive or negative) in front of others, even family members. In the individualistic US, the distinction between who is an "insider" and who an "outsider" is not so germane as in a collectivist culture. People, it seems to Hye Young, show openness to a broad array of others, even those quite different from then.

Hye Young appears to enjoy the "smiling to strangers" custom she has encountered in the US, and intends to bring it back home to Korea. This is an excellent example of a values change – seeing one's home culture with new eyes, and being permanently changed by it.

Stories on a similar theme:
Body Distance (Communication)
The Bow (Communication)

How to React to Compliments
Kay (Ikei) Kobayashi
Japan

Please read descriptions of:

Harmony and Face
Individualism and Collectivism
Modesty
Value Changes

Comment:

A goal in individualistic cultures is to raise children who are confident, self-assured, and empowered, so parents and coaches bathe children in self-esteem-building experiences. They cheer successes, even minor and imperfect ones, and look for opportunities to spotlight triumphant moments. In this context, it is acceptable for a parent to accept praise for a child without appearing arrogant, as the assumption is that it is good for the whole society for children to grow up feeling competent and skilled.

A goal in collectivist cultures is to raise children who are strong, loyal contributors to a harmonious, well-functioning group, so parents and coaches help children learn to fight against a tendency to grab attention for themselves. They praise modesty, they value the sharing of credit, and they quietly build robust, other-oriented community members. In this context, it is preferable for parents to react to a compliment by demurring, as the assumption is that it is good for the whole society if children grow up feeling quietly and inwardly respectful and strong.

In this one clear moment on the soccer field, Kay vividly captures this difference in parenting goals. Through a clear understanding of the competing goals, she herself has found a way to adapt to the challenge of living between cultures – she says one thing in response to compliments from American parents, quite another in response to Japanese ones. She notes that her son, too, appears to have internalized her Japanese values, when he shares the soccer trophy with the goalie.

After eight years of helping her children negotiate two cultures, she happily sees signs that her son's Japanese identity is strong, even when his peers are confused by his behavior. In terms of Berry's Acculturation Model, her son has taken a step from Assimilation toward Integration.

Stories on a similar theme:

Body Distance (Communication)

I Recommend Your Children Do Sports in America
Nobuko Kodama
Japan

Please read descriptions of:

Value Changes
Effort Optimism
Modesty
Individualism and Collectivism

Comment:

Although this story is written about sports, the message about how to encourage children to improve their skills is relevant to the school room as well. Nobuko writes about her joy at seeing her sons enjoy sports in the US. She is struck by the encouraging things the coaches, parents and other players say to the children, even when they have not done a perfect job. Many observers note the same thing happening in US classrooms – teachers write, "Great job!" at the top of a paper even if it has errors on it.

Americans are among the most optimistic culture in the world, especially in terms of what they believe they can control. They are more likely than most other cultures to think they control their own destinies. And the US culture facilitates people trying again after a failure – bankruptcy laws are lax, the education system allows multiple points of entry, etc. Perhaps American children learn this optimism on the ball field, as their culture cheers them on to continue trying even in the face of failure.

Nobuko sees the Japanese way – of requiring children to "cowboy up" – with new eyes, after the experience of seeing her children thrive in the US system. Some people worry that the downside of the US approach is that children do not attain the same level of expertise as they would with more negative feedback, holding them to a higher standard. Parents may have different goals for sports and for academic skills, and may, therefore, evaluate the various modes of encouragement differently in different settings.

One other unspoken value revealed in this story concerns a Japanese child's responsibility to play well for his/her team's sake – of course this is true in any team sport in any country. But the words used to encourage children to improve may differ, with coaches in individualistic countries emphasizing individual skill ("Good eye!") and those in collectivist countries emphasizing team success ("We need you to do better!"). In collectivist countries, a child who drops the ball shames the team; in individualistic one, the error reflects primarily on that child.

Stories on a similar theme:

American Courtesy (Communication)
My Struggle with Discipline and Praise (Communication)

I'm Sorry
Jong-eun Park
Korea

Please read descriptions of:

Power Distance
Harmony and Face
Burdening Others

Comment:

Jong-eun explores the nuanced meaning of the word "sorry" in different cultures and different interpersonal contexts – what does the word really mean, and who is likely to use the word? This story is a vivid illustration of how much culture and meaning can be conveyed in one single word.

That the word is used differently in Korea and the US is Jong-eun's primary point. In her experience, Americans use the term when they actually really feel sorry, and, in turn, expect forgiveness; the exchange feels simpler to her – "I did something wrong, I apologize, you forgive me, it's over." In contrast, the social rules for using the word in Korea seem complex, even to Jong-eun. She tells us that "Sorry" is more often used by people lower in a status relationship – children but not parents, citizens but not governors, younger but not older people, students but not teachers. (And she points out the Confucian root to a concern with hierarchy in interpersonal relationships.) To do so would be to admit that you had failed in your role as mentor or leader, and this, it seems to her, is the primary function of the apology – the admission of failure.

This story conveys one other interesting phenomenon – that cultural behavior can change when taken away from home. Jong-eun begins by describing how often Koreans say, "Sorry" (in America). But she then describes how they rarely use the word in Korea. The behavior – using the word "Sorry" – changes, but the value – show humility especially when in a guest or lower social status – remains the same.

Stories on a similar theme:

Apologies (Communication)

Invisibility: Upsetting and Happy Episodes in Daily Life

Mary Hsu
Taiwan

Please read descriptions of:

Value Changes
Culture Shock Cycle

Comment:

Mary shares a vivid example of one of the ways discrimination occurs – rendering someone "invisible" by attending to others deemed, possibly unconsciously, as more important. Her husband's anger and somber assessment of the reality of racism are understandable, through Mary's clear telling. Her ability to protect her own dignity and "keep her mind in purity as a mirror" is remarkable, and has allowed her to be open to those instances when people who are very different from her embrace her – by calling her "Honey" and "Sweetheart." Rather than shutting down all interactions with those who are different, she has maintained an open channel to warm human connection.

This story gives us a clear picture of how children learn values explicitly (for example, by their father's musing over the pervasiveness of racism and the importance of learning to live with those who are different) and implicitly (when they see their father's anger and solemnity, and their mother's delight at the closeness offered by the seafood clerk).

Is This a Really Good Rule?
Eriko Sasaki
Japan

Please read descriptions of:

Individualism and Collectivism
Culture Shock Cycle

Comment:

With each paragraph in this story, the reader's growing frustration matches Eriko's! She is very kind to acknowledge, up front, that there are advantages to having advanced notice about water shut offs. But haven't we all gotten caught in the foolish application of well-meaning rules?

In this incident, the problem went from superintendent to landlord's wife to landlord to plumber/handy man, and everybody in this chain stuck to the rules without looking at the whole context. Why didn't the superintendent take the problem as his own much sooner? He could have knocked on the neighbors' doors, or rigged up the gadget connecting the sink to the tub on the first day. Some combination of the high mobility rate in the US (which may have resulted in the superintendent and the residents being strangers to each other), a lack of sense of urgency on the superintendent's part, and a legalistic, individualistic "every man for himself" mentality allowed this to happen.

Probably in our own culture, we would have gone to the neighbors in the vertical column and asked if, under the circumstances, they would waive the three-day rule. But to do that with neighbors you have never met, in a foreign culture where you are uncertain of the rules, in a language that is new – that is a very different thing. In many states, tenant protection laws require landlords to fix hot water problems quickly, and allow tenants to withhold rent until the problem is fixed. But to navigate the legal and service professions may feel even more daunting than knocking on neighbors' doors. That Eriko and her family simply waited is easy to understand. This is one of those moments when lack of fluency (cultural as well as language) is overwhelmingly frustrating, more difficult, even, than taking a cold shower.

Stories on a similar theme:

Apologies (Communication)
Call Me Stupid, But Whose Responsibility is Fraud? (Cultural Adaptation)
Responsibility for Self-Management (Cultural Adaptation)
Suing and Safety (Cultural Adaptation)

Meaning of "Yes" or "No" to Answer Negative Questions
Ji-Young Choi
Korea

Please read descriptions of:

Individualism and Collectivism

Comment:

This story clearly spells out why communication problems can occur, even when people's grammar, vocabulary and syntax are excellent. Korean and English language conventions are opposite in terms of how to answer negative questions, and the results can be humorous, misleading, or worse.

The origins of this grammatical difference are unknown, but it is worth noting that in [individualistic] English, the person answering a question responds from his/her own perspective, while in [collectivist] Korean, a person answers from the perspective of the other.

Mosquitoes
Moon-Ju Kim
Korea

Please read descriptions of:

Power Distance
Effort Optimism

Comment:

Moon-Ju's dismay in this very uncomfortable situation focuses on two dimensions in which she and the camp staff had very different perceptions: (1) the seriousness of the mosquito bites, and (2) the weight her husband's letter would carry.

What linguistic and cultural barriers kept the staff from being able to reassure the Kims? What information did the Kims have that they were unable to communicate to the staff? And what role did the health risk play in all this? Perhaps nothing is more difficult for an expatriate parent than managing a child's health problem. Language problems interact with cultural differences and personal history, at a time of high anxiety, which in this case was compounded by having left the child at a sleepover camp for the first time. This is difficult for many American parents; the added stress of wondering how one's child would manage in a new language and culture is considerable. The camp personnel made the judgment that Moon-Ju's son's mosquito bites were not problematic. Was the son unable to communicate his level of discomfort to the staff (for linguistic or cultural reasons)? Did Moon-Ju and the staff hold differing beliefs about the risk of mosquito bites?

Then, Moon-Ju's frustration was made worse as she tried to redress the situation. Being sent up the ladder to people with less and less personal contact with her son was annoying, as it would be for anyone. The culture clash is clearest in her belief that her husband's letter would be sufficient evidence of an expert opinion to warrant a camp refund. The camp director was asking for an independent medical opinion that the mosquito bites warranted withdrawal from the camp. In the US, no parent, no matter how expert or accomplished, could supply the required degree of independence of judgment here, as the father's clear personal interest in the outcome would threaten to outweigh his independent opinion. In low power distance cultures like the US, priority is put on the opinions of those with no vested interest in the outcome. In contrast, in high power distance cultures like Korea, the credibility that comes with being an esteemed professor for sixteen years (even in a different medical specialty) is expected to carry more weight than independence.

Finally, Moon-Ju felt that no one from the camp apologized sufficiently to her and her family. An apology from the chief would have been very meaningful to her. In the US, especially in situations involving medical issues, staff may not apologize, for fear that an apology would connote guilt. Here, an apology seems to mean, "We did something wrong that we should not have done" rather than "We regret that your son had such an uncomfortable experience at our camp, and we wish it were not so."

Stories on a similar theme:

Apologies (Communication)
Is This a Really Good Rule? (Communication)

My Struggle with Discipline and Praise
Rieko Nozawa
Japan

Please read descriptions of:

Effort Optimism
Modesty
Value Changes

Comment:

First at a mall rest room, then in a classroom and sports field, Rieko
has noticed a practice in the US in which adults praise the kind of
behavior they want to increase, more often than they criticize or
punish children. It feels odd to Rieko, and she wonders if children
have the best opportunity for learning and for becoming strong,
under these conditions. At the same time, she sees how her son
enjoys baseball in the US and acknowledges the emotional benefits
to learning with lots of praise.

Rieko points out two moments in the Value Changes process that
are/will be challenging for her children – (1) now, having been in
the US for four years, when her "Japanese style is a little bit uncomfortable" for her children; and (2) soon, in anticipation, for when
her family returns to Japan and its very different discipline philosophy. These transitions are often difficult for children, but their
resilience typically is strong and they manage to become bicultural.
(In Berry's Acculturation Model, they will get to Integration.)

The practice of praising children is rooted in several US values.
First, Americans value the belief that, through their effort, things
will probably work out for them (effort optimism). To teach this
value, adults reinforce children's effort, sometimes even more than
their output. Saying "Good eye!" to a baseball batter who has struck
out keeps the player feeling positive and optimistic, as he can at

least be proud of his effort.

American educators and parents are also heavily influenced by experts' writings (starting in the 1960s) that emphasized "positive reinforcement" more than "punishment" as a way to guide children. Behavioral research (on animals, children and adults) supported the view that children learn more quickly and more deeply through praise and reward than through punishment. The research meshed nicely with the prevailing educational view that it is important for children to be happy, secure, confident, and optimistic learners. Still, one can easily understand Rieko's surprise at hearing a 3-year-old being praised for washing her hands!

Stories on a similar theme:

American Courtesy (Communication)
I Recommend Your Children do Sports in America (Communication)

North is Always on Top of the Map
Mina Nishimori
Japan

Please read description of:

High vs. Low Context

Comment:

Japan is generally considered to be a "high-context culture" and the US a "low-context" one. While Mina's interesting observations about maps are not an illustration of high vs. low context per se, the context element is relevant. A [low context] American map maker would not make any assumption about the user or the moment of use – which door will the walker come out of? will that ice cream store still be there? He/she would prefer to make a map that was universally usable, regardless of where the user was standing or which door he/she would use. In contrast, the [high context] Japanese map maker would prefer to stand in the shoes of the user, re-making it for those standing on this side of the station or that.

The Reason Why We are Silent
Maki Kubota
Japan

Please read descriptions of:

Individualism and Collectivism
Power Distance
Communication Style
High vs. Low Context
Harmony and Face

Comment:

Maki describes the importance she learned to put on keeping harmonious relations and of not arguing with others, especially important skills in collectivist cultures. This, she notes, is particularly important when talking to elders, as is true in cultures with higher power distance.

We can hear Maki's mother's frustration as she tried to learn what Maki, the individual, was thinking – a reminder that both individualism and collectivism exist as values, in varying degrees, in most cultures. Expatriate children who grow up juggling a home and a host culture – like the boy who was scolded by his American teacher – learn this lesson early and often.

Maki notes that a desire for harmonious relations leads Japanese people to avoid unusual dress, behavior, or ideas. In low context cultures like the US, there is little expectation that people will think or act similarly; thus, speaking up to explain or defend oneself, even to an elder, is seen as a positive skill.

Cultural differences in communication style are at play here, too. US Americans tend to put a high value on speaking clearly about what they are thinking and feeling – note the teacher's expectation that his Japanese student defend himself in Maki's story. In other cultures around the world, perhaps including Japan, more emphasis is put on communicating non-verbally, and on listening well. Americans do this too, but the balance between the importance of direct verbal communication and indirect nonverbal communication appears to differ across cultures. In the US, silence often feels awkward and Americans tend to try to fill it politely; in Japan, silence does not demand to be filled. Without understanding that this communication difference is a culturally-learned one, it is easy to make mistaken attributions about others – to assume that a person is "argumentative and disrespectful" (from one point of view) or "overly deferential" (from the other side).

Stories on a similar theme:

Apologies (Communication)
I'm Sorry (Communication)
The Bow (Communication)

Talk to Strangers
Akemi Iwai
Japan

Please read descriptions of:

Value Changes
Power Distance
Interpersonal Boundaries

Comment:

Akemi gives us a vivid picture of what it feels like to live with different rules about interpersonal boundaries. Never speaking to a neighbor, or standing in line for an hour without talking to the person next to you is an invisible way of preserving privacy, one that is perhaps especially important in a city or crowded environment. Whom you speak to (and whom you don't) also marks group membership clearly, something that feels natural in a more collectivist culture. In the US, in contrast, speaking to a stranger does not carry any meaning about group membership – it does not carry with it any implication of future involvement or obligation to the other. Individualists, with their permeable boundaries, float in and out of casual relationships without much thought to a continuing relationship.

This feels strange to Akemi, but after a conscious attempt to try it the American way, she is rewarded by a heart-warming conversation with an elderly neighbor. She anticipates a reverse culture shock when she returns to Japan.

Notice Akemi's surprise that relationships, even casual ones, can continue in the US without what feels like pertinent information to her – the other person's age and life situation. In order to use the correct vocabulary in Japanese, she needs to know if the person is older or younger than she is. The ways in which power distance affect language and relationships are striking here. In the [lower power distance] US, there may be some subtle differences in language when there is a great age discrepancy (in politeness, or deference) but not in simple vocabulary, and not between people whose age is so similar that it would require asking about.

Too Much Caring About Others' Thinking
Kay (Ikei) Kobayashi
Japan

Please read descriptions of:

Burdening Others
Harmony
Individualism and Collectivism

Comment:

Parents in the US – and perhaps in all countries – often also care what others think about their children; Japan is certainly not unique in this way. But the countries may differ, as Kay points out, in how much parents care, and in the number or kind of ways in which parents want their children to conform to a uniform standard. In the US, earlier in the 20th century, some parents and teachers did try to convert left-handed children to be right-handed, but it was not driven so much by politeness or concern for what others would think. Rather, they had a more individualistic concern that left-handedness was a disease or malfunction, and/or would be inconvenient for the child.

In collectivist cultures where harmony in human relations is a core value, children are understandably taught to be centrally concerned with how their behavior will affect others. In individualistic cultures, children are taught how to fend for themselves, a skill that will benefit them in life.

Stories on a similar theme:

Role of Shame in Parenting and Discipline (Cultural Adaptation)

Cultural Adaptation

Call Me Stupid, But Whose Responsibility is Fraud?

Japan

Please read description of:

Effort Optimism

Comment:

Yumiko's frustration is very understandable. Scams like what she describes do exist in other countries as well, but it may be that newcomers are especially vulnerable to them. People with "foreign-sounding" names or living in known immigrant communities may be targeted more by scammers. In addition, within one's own culture, one can probably spot a scam more easily than when in a new one. The language con-artists use, the things they get us to agree to, the questions they ask – all these are harder to assess in a new language and a new culture.

There is another cultural factor at play here, which Yumiko notes when she asks why victims are blamed. In international comparisons, Americans tend to score very high on effort optimism, or "internal locus of control," meaning that they tend to believe that what happens to them in life is a matter of their own actions, for better and for worse. From an internal locus of control point of view, for example, if a person gets rich, it is because he/she is either smart or has worked hard (but not because of luck or fate). The flip side of this is that when bad things happen to people, in order to be consistent with this internal locus of control, there is a tendency to blame them – as Yumiko says, if her purse was stolen, it is perceived to be because she was not careful. Cultures view blame, responsibility and luck quite differently.

Stories on a similar theme:

Is This a Really Good Rule? (Communication)
Responsibility for Self-Management (Cultural Adaptation)
Suing and Safety (Cultural Adaptation)

Deciding Whether to Move to a Foreign Country
Maki Fukunaga
Japan

Please read descriptions of:

Culture Shock Cycle
Homogeneity

Comment:

Maki was consulted as an "expert" in what it means to uproot a family to move to a new country – disrupted careers, distance from extended family, altered educational and social experience for children. She spells out in a lovely way how the choice seemed to her, while acknowledging the ways in which her situation differed from this man's. Her story highlights the many factors that influence a family's choice – the age of children, their prior experience with moves, the spouse's career. In some countries, and with some careers, taking a several-year break from a job is not a problem. In others, once a person steps off the career path, it is virtually impossible to get back on it.

Maki's comments about motivation for an overseas sojourn are also thought-provoking. She notes that most people point to the opportunity to learn English, but finds that other factors were even more compelling for her. Moving to the US offered her young children the opportunity to experience and become comfortable with people who look different, something she finds more difficult to do in Japan. She jumped at the chance to offer her children this experience, the younger the better.

And finally, Maki offers the wisdom that a few "bitter" experiences can be growth-inducing for children. To know what it is like not to be able to join with friends, or to communicate with a teacher, is a valuable lesson that she hopes will stick with them. That children can use their intercultural experience to develop long-lasting empathy is an important consideration.

Going Home Again
Chien Ju Lin
Taiwan

Please read descriptions of:
Culture Shock Cycle

Comment:

Chien Ju illuminates some of the major phases and frustrations of culture shock and reentry, which can be immensely draining and exhausting. Physical discomfort and the loss of an ability to communicate proved to be particularly salient features of culture shock for Chien Ju. It is likely that these were made more difficult by her lack of knowledge of social norms and how to accomplish practical tasks, common to all newcomers. Is this a good dentist? Is this the right school for my child? How do I open a bank account? In her home culture, she knew how to evaluate these issues, but in her host country, the rules (and language) are all different. Being forced to relearn simple tasks commonly results in feelings of incompetency, frustration, and fatigue – which easily translate to culture shock. It is natural to interpret a new country's practices as frustrating or inferior relatively to one's own, at least until they are mastered and deeply understood.

Chien Ju then gives a vivid description of what it feels like to begin, finally, to adjust to her host culture, observing some of the advantages of living in her community, such as the playgrounds, the school system, and the natural beauty. She also paints a picture of what reentry can look and feel like. Going back home can be quite challenging—sometimes even more challenging than the culture shock experienced when entering a new culture. Chien Ju shares how her home felt different from how she remembered it – it is unlikely that Taipei got more polluted (or crowded, humid or noisy) in the period Chien Ju was gone, but these characteristics went from being unexamined factors in her environment (the water a fish swims in) to being contrasted with what she experienced in the US. Interpreting one's home culture differently is a common feature of reentry.

Stories on a similar theme:

The Picture of Homeland (Cultural Adaptation)

Hurry Up
Inhee Ryou
Korea

Please read descriptions of:

Burdening Others
Wastefulness

Comment:

Many many people have been frustrated by the pace at their local Registry of Motor Vehicles. Still, there is no cultural excuse for poor service, as Inhee got. But why does the US tolerate this kind of service when it would not be tolerated in Korea?

The US does not represent the polar extreme in terms of speed and efficiency. Many European have noted, in fact, the *fast* pace of Americans - always rushing, drinking coffee on the go rather than sitting in a café with a friend, eating lunch at your desk while working, etc. In Korea, the standard business employee gets about one week's vacation; in the US there is no central control but the norm is 2-3 weeks. Six weeks is standard in some parts of Europe.

Time sense is one of the most deeply-learned cultural senses, and therefore re-setting one's clock is one of the most difficult adjustments to make in another culture.

Making Friends
Kay (Ikei) Kobayashi
Japan

Please read descriptions of:

Homogeneity
Burdening Others
Individualism and Collectivism
Modesty

Comment:

Kay describes her eager willingness to transcend cultural differences and make friends despite different customs and expectations. She has easily adjusted her behavior – no more snacks for play dates, stepping into the friend's home for a tour – even while noting that these are actions that carry heartfelt meaning for her. Giving up the sense of being a good [gift-bearing] guest, and overcoming what feels like a lack of modesty to enter the private spaces of someone's home – these kinds of changes don't happen without a core sense of openness and flexibility. Kay's experience of being a kind of outsider even in Japan (with her non-Japanese-style name), may have facilitated her openness to difference in the US.

It is these subtle differences in what Kay calls "common sense" (or we might call "cultural values") that often make it difficult to make friends across cultures. As Kay notes, problems with English are relatively easily overcome, once a level of proficiency is reached. What is harder is making friends across a gap of differing values. Kay feels most comfortable sending a snack with her son on a play date, but she has gotten the feedback that Americans don't feel the same way. Perhaps they feel that if she does that, then they would be required to send a thoughtful snack when the play date is reciprocated, and Americans might prefer not to enter into this cycle of obligation. Individualists, in general, tend to navigate their interpersonal relationships in ways that minimize complex, long-standing interconnections. So just in this one small habit, we see a range and depth of cultural differences. Developing a friendship requires the navigation of many such habits and assumptions, and it is no wonder that many people report difficulty in making friends with people from other cultures.

Stories on a similar theme:

Making Friends with Americans
Starting a Friendship with Americans in the US

On the Street
Soo-kyeung Park
Korea

Please read descriptions of:

Culture Shock Cycle
Value Changes

Comment:

In the course of this one short story, Soo-kyeong takes us on quite an emotional journey, from her frightened, timid arrival on a dark and snowy night, to a mind set of seeing her own and her new culture in a balanced and optimistic way.

Everyone who moves to Boston can certainly identify with Soo-kyeung's reaction to driving in this city, where a yellow light means "hurry up" and a red light is a mere suggestion. But note that Soo-kyeong goes immediately to a critique of the driving in Seoul – they aren't careful of pedestrians and they don't pull over for ambulances. The way drivers in these two cultures are crazy is different, but Soo-kyeung seems to weigh these differences in a balanced way. "This I like, this I don't."

Living in her new culture gets Soo-kyeung to examine her own culture with new eyes. She re-thinks Stop signs and ambulance protocol. These are the experiences that make crossing cultures so interesting and, when it's time to return home, unsettling.

Soo-kyeung also reflects thoughtfully on the personal strengths that newcomers must use to move to a new culture. She finds strength she did not know she had, in overcoming shyness and lack of experience.

Parent-Child Relationships in the USA
Tomoko Shimizu
Japan

Please read descriptions of:
Culture Shock Cycle
Value Changes
Individualism and Collectivism
Power Distance

Comment:

Tomoko writes beautifully about her struggle to raise her daughter in a way that honors her own values yet releases her to embrace American culture as well. In terms of Berry's Acculturation model, she is describing a sadness that her daughter is in Assimilation (rejecting her parents' Japanese cultural norms). Tomoko openly wants her daughter to be "American" but it still feels like a loss to her, as her daughter adopts more American values than she does herself.

She understands her daughter's course as being influenced by conflicting values: the respect for traditions she wishes her to have (as is common in high power distance cultures) vs. respect for newness her daughter seems to be adapting (more common in low power distance cultures like the US). She looks back at US history to try to understand the immigrant experience and, in doing so, joins millions who have walked before her on this path.

She is at the same time proud of her daughter's explosive English proficiency and sad at the gulf she sees growing between them, fueled both by linguistic and cultural experience. She is sad to think that she can't be an emulated model for her daughter if her goal is for her daughter to become an American. It feels as if that part of her role as parent has been lost to her.

This experience is all rather new for Tomoko and her family. As her daughter continues to develop and live in two cultures, it is likely that her daughter will become bicultural (or in Integration, in Berry's terms). She will be able to honor her parents' traditions, look to them as models, and speak their language (literally and metaphorically) and be able to navigate the American world as well.

Of course, many parents, even those raising their children in their own culture, struggle with their children's growing independence of thought. As children grow into adolescence and young adulthood, especially in individualistic cultures like the US, parents may have to face the reality that their children have different ideas and goals than they have. This process is compounded for families living in global transition.

Stories on a similar theme:

How to React to Compliments (Communication)

The Picture of Homeland
Ying-Ying Chen
Taiwan

Please read descriptions of:

Culture Shock Cycle
Value Changes

Comment:

Ying-Ying describes, with clarity and honesty, the ways her view of
her home country waxed and waned with time and distance. First
vivid longing; then memories dissolving in the face of a busy life in
the US; then, with just the thought of a visit home, a return of the
vivid expectations – and finally a dose of reality on arrival – "the
food was just ordinary and general...good, just as it should be, but
not dreamlike." She includes some wonderful examples of the kind
of perceptual distortion that so often happens in remembering –
the size of her mother's house, the safety of drivers, the cleanness
of the air – and the jolt one feels when encountering reality.

Ying-Ying also shares an example of a value change she had under-
gone while living in the US – that of child care. One can imagine
the adjustment people from her culture might have to make, upon
arriving in the US, to shift from being a busy career woman whose
baby was tended during the week outside her home, to caring for a
2-year-old all day long, and then to shift to seeing the advantages of
a different way.

Stories on a similar theme:

Going Home Again (Cultural Adaptation)

Responsibility for Self-Management
Kiyoko Kijima
Japan

Please read description of:

Effort Optimism

Comment:

Kiyoko highlights the ways that one simple value – the belief that one can control one's own destiny – affects so many aspects of life. It is not that Americans consciously say, "Well, I am in charge of my own destiny so I don't mind when telephone companies over charge me – hey, I'll check my bill, catch it, and take care of it." But they do allow a system to develop that reveals these underlying beliefs. Better to have the occasional telephone spam problem than to allow the government or utility company too much access to one's private records, says the prevailing American belief – and so telephone spamming continues, even if illegal and punished.

In the medical domain, Kiyoko observes Americans actually showing up for cancer screenings, behaving in a way that suggests they believe they control their destiny – "I'm doing my part to control my life by having this test." In fact, this core US belief sometimes makes it especially difficult for Americans who do develop serious illnesses, so unaccustomed are they to the sense of helplessness and lack of control that some illnesses present.

Stories on a similar theme:

Is This a Really Good Rule? (Communication)
Call Me Stupid, But Whose Responsibility is Fraud? Cultural Adaptation)
Suing and Safety (Cultural Adaptation)

Role of Shame in Parenting and Discipline
Susumu Kobayashi
Japan

Please read descriptions of:

Individualism and Collectivism
Burdening Others
Harmony and Face

Comment:

We see here how a concern with Face gets transmitted within a culture. Susumu made his mother lose face when he cried in the toy store ("Look, people are looking and laughing at us"). While individualistic parents are surely embarrassed by crying children in toy stores, too, what they say to their children (and so what value is explicitly being taught) is more likely to focus on the child as an individual ("[You should] Stop it! People are looking at you."). A child's responsibility for his mother's face is not articulated.

In general, individualistic cultures are thought to emphasize guilt more than shame, and collectivist cultures shame more than guilt. As Susumu explains, the shame he was taught as a child required the presence (and importance) of other people – the other people in the store, or the others in his group, family, or community. If they weren't there to witness the problem behavior, that element of shame would not exist. Guilt, in contrast, can be felt all alone – even if no one in your community knows you did something wrong, you know it and can feel guilty.

Susumu rightly points out that this is a distinction that is not a pure one – his parents internalized a sense of shame by teaching him to imagine other people watching him. And surely many Western parents ask their children, "What will the neighbors think?" as a shame-inducing parenting device.

Still, parents in individualistic cultures are more likely to take pride in children who buck the trend, or stand out from the crowd. This is especially clear in the comparison of the importance of "not troubling others" vs. "being respected by others." The collectivist goal is to not be a burden to others; the individualistic goal is to stand out from others and be respected (presumably for one's individual accomplishments).

Stories on a similar theme:

Too Much Caring About Others' Thinking (Communication)

Starting a Friendship with Americans in the US
Su-Pin, Liao (Ping)
Taiwan

Please read descriptions of:

Communication Style
Culture Shock Cycle

Comment:

Ping gives us a very clear picture of her experience in trying to make friends across cultures. She rightly notes the benefits of having a common language – although some good friendships have developed across language barriers too, sometimes with the help of common non-linguistic interests like music or sports, or through shared commitment to a cause or activity.

Ping notes that it is not just having English capability that is important in developing a friendship, but also an understanding of communication style differences. These communication style rules are usually unspoken, like how much silence to tolerate before filling it, which kinds of topics are OK and which are taboo, and whether words – expressing one's feelings verbally – are diamonds or not. Even native English speakers must struggle with these kinds of

160

communication style differences in the US.

Another aspect of American friendships that Ping encounters is one of expectations. Americans call a person a "friend" after they have met in their children's school yard a few times, or are in the same class, or live near each other. Ping reserves the word "friend" for someone intimately involved in her life – someone to talk to about money, marriage, and jobs.

And finally, Ping points out vividly the important of being in a place where friendships with host nationals have a chance of developing – having an available social network. There were, of course, no Americans in her English classes, and she looked forward to meeting American peers at her new graduate program. Of course, friendships with others from one's home or other culture can be deeply meaningful and helpful while living in another country, and are a common source of social support for most people living in a new country. But Ping's focus here is on the access to her host culture – the US, in this case – that one derives from having host culture friends.

Stories on a similar theme:

Making Friends
Making Friends with Americans

Suing and Safety
Hyeyoung Yoon
Korea

Please read descriptions of:

Effort Optimism
High vs. Low Context
Individualism and Collectivism

Comment

There are several core cultural issues underlying the litigiousness of US culture. The tendency to sue seems, on its face, selfish to a collectivist – so much attention on one person's need, ignoring the surrounding context. In addition, we see in this example Americans' belief that they have control over what happens to them. They assume credit for their successes and place blame on themselves or others when something goes wrong. Little is attributed to "fate." If someone slips and falls on some ice, it must be someone's fault, and if it is someone's fault, that person should have to make amends.

Another underlying cultural issue is the sheer number of lawyers in the US (which then makes it relatively accessible to consider suing someone), a result in part of the US being a low context culture. In low context cultures, one cannot assume what another person thinks or understands or believes or trusts; in the US, this low context feature arose from Americans coming from widely varying subcultures and from their being raised in the belief of their own uniqueness. If one cannot make assumptions about others, then it is best to write everything down clearly, and to agree to obey the written word. And for that, many lawyers are needed.

The litigiousness of US culture – especially the hot coffee example – is apparently well known around the world; usually we hear that it is poorly regarded. It may surprise the reader to hear Hyeyoung's reminder that there's a positive side to our law-suit-happy society. If people work to improve safety because they don't want to be sued, at least there is increased safety as a benefit.

Stories on a similar theme:

Is This a Really Good Rule? (Communication)
Call Me Stupid, But Whose Responsibility is Fraud? Cultural Adaptation)

The Word You Won't See in a Dictionary
Anonymous
Japan

Comment:

This story provides a vivid and heart-wrenching example of what it is like to go through the process of becoming fully fluent in a culture, including its hidden corners. Slang expressions and idioms are difficult to learn, and dictionaries may not be helpful if they give technical definitions. The Girl Scout and the writer's daughter both got caught in that little space between fluency and Really Not Knowing – had the girls been not quite so good at English, they wouldn't have been in the position of taking notes and minutes for the group. They had picked up many subtleties of English (intonation, pitch) by copying what they heard, but the illicitness of the words in question somehow was not signaled to them until it was too late.

Note that the writer's daughter looked the word up in an English dictionary, not a Japanese-English one – a further sign of her fluency. The contrast between the girl's skill and her mistake must have added to her shock and confusion, cold water on a sunny day. Further, the writer shares with us the empathy she feels for her daughter as she encounters the shaming taunts of her peers, and her own frustration of not being able to help.

Customs

Barrier-free
Satoko Takahashi
Japan

Please read descriptions of:

Value Changes
Individualism and Collectivism

Comment:

One striking aspect about this story is Satoko's distress at the interaction she witnessed when visiting her home culture after living outside it for several years. She now sees the treatment of a person with a disability as demeaning in a way she might not have noticed before living in the [individualistic] US. Hofstede (2005) has noted that collectivistic cultures tend to treat people with disabilities (and other differences) as shameful. Satoko's US experience orients her to be sensitive to the person's disability in a new way.

Satoko teaches us, through this story, a bit about why "you can't go home again" – after living in another culture, one is affected by the experience in ways that make it impossible to fit neatly back into one's previous home. Although surprised at first at the US bathroom and the parking provisions made for people with disabilities, she clearly came to understand both the practical and the social barriers that societies must eliminate. And so, returning home, she was watching her culture (and its barrier-free movement) with Americanized eyes. There, she was incensed that the man she met in the Japanese shop was apologizing to her rather than simply thanking her – how was this his fault? Not incensed at the man, of course, but at the social value and assumption that she now saw very differently. This is what happens when you live in a new culture and then go home.

Stories on a similar theme:

Apologies (Communication)

Birthday Parties
Mary Hsu
Taiwan

Please read descriptions of:

Individualism and Collectivism

Comments:

Mary's observations of the common American tradition of the birthday party provide a close look at some deep-rooted US values. In the US, a birthday party is a celebration of the unique qualities of one person, a time for the birthday child to be special among his/her friends and family. Setting aside and honoring this moment teaches and reflects a key US American value of individualism. Conversely, Mary, who grew up in a collectivistic culture, offers a very different perspective. Instead of feeling the urge to celebrate herself on her birthday, she has a natural instinct to thank and honor her mother for "bringing [her] into the world and raising [her]." She wonders whether Americans also have birthday parties for their own parents. This story eloquently outlines the US focus on the individual (starting from one's very first birthday), as opposed to the typically collectivistic focus on the family, relationships, and group.

Another interesting point evidenced in this story is the tendency for consumerism and what feels to Mary like frivolous spending in US culture. Mary expresses her discomfort with American parents spending excessive money and energy on a child's birthday party. The goody bags, the decorations, the balloons and, the last straw, the new socks for all – these felt over the top to Mary. That this spending was focused on an individual, and a child at that, adds to her discomfort. In contrast, individualistic/American parents enjoy the chance to shower attention (and gifts) on each child, trusting that each child will have his/her "day" in the spotlight.

The Culture of Dumping
Hyeyoung Yoon
Korea

Please read descriptions of:
Choice
Wastefulness

Comment:

The global nature of the importance of energy conservation and pollution control is becoming clear to Americans. Since Hyeyoung wrote this story, the community where she lived in the US has started to consider the kinds of trash pickup system she described in Korea, and re-usable grocery bags have become very popular.

Still, the US has a long way to go in institutionalizing change.

Another cultural obstacle to environmental change in the US is American's tendency to prefer having personal choice in how they lead their lives, resisting centralized governmental control whenever possible. Regulations that require people to dispose of trash in a certain way or that prohibit paper and plastic cups run counter to this sense of individual freedom.

Stories on a similar theme:

School Lunch (Education)
Unnecessary Electricity (Customs)

Family Advice about Pregnancy
Michelle Su
Taiwan

Please read descriptions of:

Power Distance
Individualism and Collectivism

Comment:

In this story Michelle shares a great example of power distance. She, as well as many other mothers from her culture, follows the rules of *zho-yeh-tz* because it is a respected tradition that is encouraged and passed down from mothers and mother-in-laws. Although there are parts of the tradition that she (or other mothers) may disagree with, out of respect for the older generation, she follows, or pretends to follow the rules anyway. It is this deference to tradition and respected elders that illustrates the concept of high power distance.

Michelle also shares her difficulty adjusting to certain cultural norms around childbirth. Not only does she "pretend" with her mother, but also with the nurses caring for her! Her struggle between adhering to the cultural norms of her native country, and those of the US was illustrated in her example of messing up the towels so the nurse would believe that she had taken a shower. In fact, the emotional struggle was so strong that it may have contributed to Michelle blacking out when, against her cultural norm, she was pressured into exercising after her delivery.

Michelle also points out the pressure and burden she felt to provide a baby boy in order to continue her husband's blood line. In the current US context, where gender equality and low power distance are common cultural values, this shared familial and social pressure to produce a son (rather than a daughter) would be muted or deemed inappropriate and sexist.

Feet on the Seat
Chi-Chen Chou
Taiwan

Please read descriptions of:

Formality and Informality
Individualism and Collectivism
Value Changes

Comment:

Many Americans say they also dislike the habit of people putting feet on the chair in front of them. But why does it occur in the US anyway, and not Taiwan?

Part of the US emphasis on informality is a casualness about decorum in public places. Here, Chi-Chen notes her discomfort with what seems to her to be an unsanitary and intrusive informal practice, putting feet on a seat in a theater. This habit could also be perceived as rather egocentric – while it may be comfortable to the student behind, it completely ignores the fact that a foot is within inches of a stranger's face.

This story is a vivid example of the cultural nature of personal boundaries and space. Chi-Chen finds it uncomfortable that someone has "invaded" her personal bubble or space – particularly with a foot near her face. This is all the more striking because, in general, Chinese people are more comfortable with less interpersonal space than US Americans – they may stand closer together while talking, for example, If the student were putting her arms on the chair rather than her feet, it might not be so bad. But in a culture where people take shoes off when entering a house, placing one's feet near someone's face is intolerable.

She makes a point of instructing her children not to adopt this American practice, framing her request as a traditional Chinese one. Her children receive two messages – a traditional Chinese one from a parent and an individualistic one, by example, from their American peers. This poses a classic bicultural conflict that children living in a new culture must face.

Gift Giving in Return
Kay (Ikei) Kobayashi
Japan

Please read descriptions of:
Individualism and Collectivism
Burdening Others
Modesty

Comment:

Some cultures have stricter rules about gift giving than others; Japan's rules are more explicit than rules in the US – even if younger people think they are "ridiculous," as Kay suggests. Much has been written about gift-giving in Japan – what combination of debt, loyalty, kindness and/or love is being expressed with a gift, for example? Which gifts (of what value, from whom, given under what occasions) must be reciprocated, and which do not require a return gift? What is communicated in how the gift is wrapped? This aspect of Japanese culture is beyond the scope of this book, but the overarching issue of the explicitness and strictness of social rules can be examined in general cultural terms.

In collectivist cultures, the rules of conduct within a group are generally enforced by social sanction and moral force. One obeys the rules to be a "good" person – in Kay's case, one gives a half return to show that one is modest and honors custom, and to even up any imbalance in obligation or burden. There is stability, and therefore harmony and peace, when this kind of balance is achieved. In contrast, in individualistic cultures, the context of gift giving is less dominant. People pick a gift they think will appeal, within a generally-normative price range, with no expectation of a return gift. (Or at least an immediate return gift is not expected. Some general accounting over time may be expected – if you give my son a graduate gift this June, I will probably give your daughter one next June when she graduates.)

Golden Week
Akiko Ohashi
Japan

Please read descriptions of:

Homogeneity
High vs. Low Context
Choice

Comment:

It is impossible to know how a custom like the one Akiko describes – most people taking vacation on the same days – developed. But concern about not being at work when "everyone else" is – a common concern in homogeneous cultures, where being different is rare – would certainly motivate the custom. This story provides a fine example of how control over decisions differs across cultures – from being quite centralized in Japan (the government sets the 15 days holiday and most people – by choice but also by cultural pressure – take vacations then) to decentralized in the US (with fewer holidays that are observed throughout the country, and vacations spread out over several good-weather months).

Stories on a similar theme:

Being Absent from School (Education)

Korean Daughter-in-Law
Meesuk Kang
Korea

Please read descriptions of:

Individualism and Collectivism
Power Distance
Homogeneity
Burdening Others
Value Changes

Comment:

Meesuk offers a wonderfully clear picture of the implications of living in a collectivist, high power distance culture. She spells out just what her role responsibilities are (especially to elders), and how she came to learn them – from parents and teachers, from Confucius, from her sisters-in-law. Low power distance, individualist children are encouraged to do well in school, too, but it is for their own benefit, not explicitly so their class will be first or their family famous.

The idea of a culture having a widely-accepted norm for which children will care for elderly parents, or who will be close to whom, will sound foreign to low-power-distance readers. For those in individualistic, low power distance cultures, elder care will depend on a variety of factors – proximity, personal closeness, and financial ability, for example. The idea that "married daughters will belong to their husband's family" goes against the low power distance value of egalitarianism. Even using a broad definition of "belonging to" that includes "feeling especially close to," in low power distance cultures, there is no broad acceptance that women will join their husband's family. Proximity, personality and preference play a stronger role than gender in determining couples' alliances and relationships.

Meesuk makes the interesting observation that since all Korean girls and young women hear the same messages about what sisters, daughters and students should do, they are more similar to each other than women in the US. She is highlighting one concrete way a culture becomes homogeneous in some ways.

When she writes, "I am sure it is definitely right…" for children to care for their parents, it seems she may be mulling this issue over, with the distance of several thousand miles and a glimpse at the individualistic way Americans care for their parents. (In individualistic cultures, parents are more likely to feel proud of their children's independence from them, and make retirement plans that specifically keep them from being "a burden" on their children.) Meesuk acknowledges the burden she sometimes feels, and worries about who will take care of parents without sons.

Meesuk arrived in the US with a strong collectivist sense of loyalty and obligation to her parents-in-law, she examined that value from a distance, and she returned to it. While her fundamental belief has not changed, she apparently sees it in a new light by virtue of having lived in a new and very different culture.

Play Dates
Maki Kubota
Japan

Please read descriptions of:

Individualism and Collectivism

Comment:

It is important to note that the kind of informal play arrangements Maki recalls in Japan are also common in some parts of the US, though not in the Boston suburb where she lived. There, parental cautiousness and safety concerns do influence the age at which children are allowed to walk home from school by themselves or with friends. A high proportion of families with two working parents in that community also means that at-home supervision is sometimes provided by a paid babysitter or a parent working in the home, which may complicate plans to invite other children to play. Some parents may be uncertain enough of a child's at-home supervision that they will want to be involved in any plans that happen there. The children's many after-school activities and lessons also involve complex scheduling and chauffeuring, which are then in place for the occasional free afternoon; hence the more formal play date gets scheduled in a way that strikes Maki as odd.

Maki makes an interesting observation that American families in her US community more commonly arrange for play dates with just one other child (rather than a small group), and that the American parents intervene in disagreements or conflicts more readily than in Japan. Each culture is thereby providing its children with a training ground for instilling a core value – individualism in the US and collectivism in Japan. By keeping the group small (two children), the American parents are maximizing the chance for each child to have his/her own needs met, and contextually minimizing the opportunity for conflict. When conflict does arise, the American parents are more concerned with solving the problem (even if they have to do it themselves) than giving the children the social chance to sort things out themselves. In contrast, the Japanese parents, inviting larger groups, are providing the opportunity for the children to encounter and solve problems and deal with competing needs, especially important skills in a collectivist society.

Stories on a similar theme:

Receiving Visitors (Customs)

Receiving Visitors
Jong-eun Park
Korea

Please read descriptions of:

Individualism and Collectivism
Harmony and Face
Culture Shock Cycle
Value Changes

Comment:

The image of Jong-eun's son telling her to do snacks the American way is a good illustration of how important it is for children to find a way to fit in at that early stage of the relocation cycle (which Berry calls Assimilation). Only later can children appreciate their bicultural skills and be proud to show off a different way of being to their host national friends.

Probably Jong-eun's son's chip-providing friend wasn't very hungry that afternoon, and assumed his guest wasn't either. The relationship between guests and hosts is not so formalized in the US. American parents are more likely to leave their children to get after-school snacks for themselves and their guests. While the parents hope their children remember to consider their guests' desires, they may not take the kind of care of guests that Jong-eun describes. If American children want to eat more, they may say, "Hey, I'm hungry!" Americans communicate, in their individualistic way, "Take what you want, for yourself, and I'll do the same." They consider the open kitchen a form of hospitality. While the American way feels stark when put this way, it is part of an individualistic cultural system that promotes a level playing field where people take care of their own needs.

Jong-eun illustrates the notion of face clearly when she notes that sometimes, "visitors suffer when they have to eat something served even though they are not hungry." If a host has gone to the trouble of making food for you, you would make them lose face by turning it down. Especially where having enough food to share is a sign of success and wealth, turning down an offer of food is to reject this important statement of identity.

Stories on a similar theme:

Play Dates (Customs)

Slumber Party

Mary Hsu

Taiwan

Please read descriptions of:

Individualism and Collectivism
Communication Style
Interpersonal Boundaries
Value Changes

Comment:

Mary beautifully describes her unfolding realization that a value she accepted from her father might not be one she wants to continue to instill in her children. This is a lovely example of how values can change while living in a new culture. Her delight at seeing something in a new way shines through in this story. She brings a viewpoint to the US, one molded by her father, about neighborhood children being a burden on other families. She encounters a startling new way of thinking about this through her daughter's slumber party invitation. She contemplates the roots of her own belief – and remembers that she didn't like her father's rule. She gives the new way a try by letting her daughter go to a trusted friend's house (with dumplings – just in case she is right about the burden part). And then she jumps in herself and invites girls to her house – "But I did, I had a slumber party..." – and she sees the issue of burden in a new light, balanced by the benefit of getting to know one's daughter and her world in a deeper way. (Although she does not write about this, it is possible that the American family did not go to so much trouble after all, what with a different view point about honoring guests.)

Mary's father – and his strong looks, his big eyes and his newspaper clippings – convey vividly just how powerful non-verbal communication can be. And when he used words – "Is there no bed for you in our own house?" – they were an indirect but extremely clear answer to her question. There was no confusion about his point of view.

Mary's father also teaches us something about how children learn who is in one's group in a collectivist culture, and who is not. A thick boundary clearly sat between Mary's and Geng's families. We cannot tell from this story who else besides Mary and her father were in their group, but clearly, Geng was not. When Mary contemplated crossing over a boundary into a new family's space (by allowing participation in slumber parties), she carried with her the notion that she would now have a complex relationship built on obligation with the other parents, a potentially daunting notion. Individualistic Americans may be more casual in their invitation to have children sleep over, as it would not carry any connotation of sustained obligation.

In fact, individualistic parents may give their children more say in who their friends will be than collectivist parents, celebrating their independence of thought. Within the limits of safety and distance, individualistic children are given a rather free hand to pick friends, whereas collectivist parents (at least traditional ones like Mary's father) offer more guidance), conveying the sense that they know best what is good for a child.

Stories on a similar theme:

Receiving Visitors (Customs)
Play Dates (Customs)

Two Thoughts about Babysitting
Kay (Ikei) Kobayashi
Japan

Please read descriptions of:

Individualism and Collectivism
Burdening Others
Value Changes
Interpersonal Boundaries

Comment:

At what age do we begin to learn our culture's values? This story helps clarify exactly how young – in infancy, in fact. Kay notes that her American peers leave their children with [paid, outside-the-family, teenage] babysitters – Americans thus begin the process of individuation, or separating the individual from the family, a key step on the route toward becoming an individualist. They value time alone with their spouse – as adults, without children, one generation alone – so much that they are willing to entrust their children to a baby sitter. While American families value having a stable, known, mature, and loving baby sitter, this option is not always available because of the mobility of the American population. It is not so common to live very close to grandparents; paid babysitters themselves may move frequently too. While many American grandparents value the opportunity to care for their grandchildren, many others make lifestyle choices that preclude this. And so the teenage babysitter is seen as an acceptable alternative. The nuclear family is key in the US.

In contrast, Kay and her Japanese peers feel more comfortable tending their own children or, if necessary, asking for help from family members, including grandparents and older siblings. Spending time alone with one's spouse takes a lower priority than fulfilling one's role as parent; in fact, Kay speaks of feeling guilty leaving her children with a babysitter unless it is a business necessity. In contrast to the picture of the American family setting its children on a course of individuation, we get a picture of a whole family working together to support a child's development within the family. Life decisions get made toward this end – including, in Kay's case, choosing to live near her parents. The extended family is key in Japan.

Kay's parents are not available to care for her children while she is in the US, and she has found a Japanese baby sitter for special circumstances. She thus has had to change her custom in response to living in a new country; it is not clear whether her values about baby sitting have changed, however. This is one of the challenges of global living – to have new customs necessitated by new circumstances that may challenge one's values.

Unnecessary Electricity
Ryoko Okazaki
Japan

Please read descriptions of:

Choice
Wastefulness

Comment:

Ryoko notices several differences in how electric power is used for the acts of daily living – laundry, washing dishes, and heating. While there is a [relatively new] environmental consciousness in the US, it is still quite common to dry clothes, wash dishes, leave lights burning, and heat homes without too much thinking about the ecological consequences of how we do so.

Ryoko does a sensitive job of making a criticism about American life, framed as a cultural issue and in the context of her general delight about living in the US. Her description of *mottainai* highlights the complexity of values within a culture. In fact, thriftiness and frugality are pioneer values from the seventeenth and eighteenth centuries, part of the American value system. (These are counterbalanced, though, by the sense of plenitude and availability of resources that the pioneers experienced, and also contributed to the US values.) There are several well-known proverbs in the US that focus on these values – "A penny saved is a penny earned," and "Necessity is the mother of invention" come close to the notion of *mottainai*, not wasting resources. But there is no single word for the concept in English, suggesting that it plays a different role in the US than in Japan.

Stories on a similar theme:

Apologies (Communication)
The Culture of Dumping (Customs)
School Lunch (Education)

Valentine's Day
Kay (Ikei) Kobayashi
Japan

Please read descriptions of:

Individualism and Collectivism

Comment:

This Western holiday has made a cultural jump to Japan, with some interesting adaptations. While in the US, gift-giving is either mutual or male-focused (flowers, candy, dates – traditionally, these "should" be instigated by the thoughtful man, not woman), in Japan it starts with the women; men have another month to figure out how to reply and whether to reciprocate an affectionate message or not.

In addition, the Japanese celebration reflects that culture's comfort with "obligation" to a group. Women must spend time and money preparing "obligatory chocolate" for their co-workers, in addition to their special chocolate gift. US classrooms have, in fact, instituted a similar convention whereby the teacher urges children to get a card for everyone. Still, the US version feels easier to Kay.

Education

Are You Coming to My Conference, Dad?
A Mother's View: Mami Kato

Are You Coming to My Conference, Dad?
A Father's Reply: Anonymous
Japan

Please read descriptions of:

Value Changes

Comment:

For international families, there are practical reasons for newcomers wanting their spouse to attend a school conference – there are an overwhelming number of cultural differences they must interpret and, in some cases, their spouse's English is better than theirs. Cultural values and gender norms influence how and whether this happens, however.

Gender role expectations differ from culture to culture, and are typically a source of surprise to newcomers to any new country. In this pair of stories, the families are faced with a community norm in which fathers engage in what is, to their Japanese expectation, a mother's job. They use the experience to explore their own values about what kind of parents they want to be.

One of the many interesting issues to arise from this story is how norms and values that we accept easily at home get called into question in a new country. In Japan, attending such a conference would be primarily the mother's job (although this is changing and some fathers attend too). Decisions about parental involvement in school are not solely up to the family, of course; businesses and schools, as part of the greater community, generally give a supporting message. For example, businesses in some countries do not allow employees to be absent to attend a school conference, and schools do not offer conferences during off-work hours.

In moving to this particular US community, parents and children get exposed to a different perspective – that having the father attend the parent-teacher conference allows both parents to be involved and to ask different questions. It also signals to both the teacher and the child that the father is involved and interested. Employers (at least in this community of generally professional-level families) agree and permit fathers to be absent for school conferences. And the school, committed to this value of parental involvement, offers some evening-hour conferences for those who cannot attend during the day.

Of course Japanese fathers care deeply about their children's education, too, but whether going to a parent-teacher conference is part of their "parenting portfolio" or not is apparently culturally influenced.

Being Absent from School
Meesuk Kang
Korea

Please read descriptions of:

Individualism and Collectivism
Value Changes

Comment:

Depending on the nature of the trip and the length of absence, many US teachers (especially in the lower grades) will agree that a trip is an opportunity for education that children should be allowed to experience. (Such trips should always be discussed with teachers ahead of time; parents are not completely free to take their children out of school in order to travel.) In the US, educators often take a broad view of what is "educational" – beyond learning directly from teachers, they include discussions, experimentation, false starts, play, creative exploration, and … travel, in the experiences that are likely to educate a child.

Note Meesuk's attention to the feelings of the teacher of an absent child: "…if a child is absent from school, parents will be sorry for the teacher, as if their child hasn't done his duty." The collectivist emphasis on reciprocal obligation and loyalty is clear here, but probably a surprise to individualists' ears, who might worry about a child's lost learning during an absence, but probably not about his/her duty to the teacher.

Similarly, note Meesuk's comments about sick children seeming to be well enough to manage staying in school. Korean [collectivist] children are asked to stick it out, learning endurance and perseverance, while American [individualistic] children are asked to go home and get well efficiently. The collectivist school group is willing to put up with the chance of germs from one of their own, just as a family (even in individualistic cultures) may not quarantine a sick child completely from the rest of the family. We see the concept of "group" beyond family illustrated clearly here.

In Meesuk's last paragraph, she notes that she understands and appreciates the American approach to school absence, but finds that her values are deeply rooted and not easily transplanted. She hears words coming out of her mouth, from her deepest self, even though at one level she likes the US attitude about school absence. Especially for families living a bicultural life, old and new ways struggle mightily with each other.

Clean Up Time
Mayumi Toyoda
Japan

Please read description of:

Individualism and Collectivism

Comment:

In this account, Mayumi is struck by the different expectations placed on American vs. Japanese school children. In Japan, children are responsible for cleaning the space they use. First, Mayumi discusses how cleaning the classroom teaches the important skill of cooperation. Next, she points out how it fosters effective communication and problem-solving skills among group members. Finally, she shares how students learn the practical or "right" way of cleaning which is part of a process. She also explains how this practice promotes a sense of responsibility, because when children are required to clean their messes, they will be less inclined to make them. All of these points are associated with certain values shared by collective cultures. Working as a group to accomplish what is necessary, and adhering to the "right way" of completing a task, are integral to living in a collective culture. Mayumi offers a clear example of how this value is transmitted to children.

For Americans, the idea of having small children do the work of a janitor is quite foreign. In American schools, children are taught to clean their own desks and personal space, but not the common space. This practice highlights the individual's responsibility to his/her self, as opposed to the larger group. Rather than learning some universal "common way," finding a creative or different way to complete this or other tasks would most likely be encouraged as a healthy form of self-expression in an American classroom. In most American classrooms, children are also encouraged to learn social skills such as cooperation, but this is likely to occur in the context of school projects, recess or sports. They are also likely to have chores at home – setting the table, making their bed, cleaning their room.

Stories on a similar theme:

School Lunch (Education)

Examination Hell in Japan
Nobuko Kodama
Japan

Please read descriptions of:

Individualism and Collectivism
Effort Optimism
Values Changes

Comment:

Here, we see an example of how Japanese and American cultural values have shaped educational choices that one parent has made for her child, depending on the context.

In Japan there is a well-defined hierarchical system that determines how people move ahead. This is often defined through family connections and access/entry to the top educational institutions. In the US, each individual is expected to succeed both academically and professionally on their own, regardless of family connections and predetermined hierarchical systems. Many Americans prefer to believe that if you just try hard enough, you will prevail. (Colleges and universities that offer preferential admissions to alumni children are a controversial exception to this value.)

Nobuko has demonstrated her bicultural understanding by flexibly shifting her approach to her child's education depending on the context. In Japan she followed the educational model that catered to Japanese cultural values, while in the US context she adopted a model that reflects US culture and values.

Learning Math and How to Think
Chinatsu Kamei
Japan

Please read descriptions of:
Value Changes
Individualism and Collectivism
Homogeneity

Comment:

Chinatsu goes beneath the surface in her observation about how math is taught, beyond just technique differences, to note that there is a fundamental difference in approach – an emphasis on practice and drilling in Japan, and an emphasis on understanding the thought process (and indeed, even inventing a new one) in the US.

Chinatsu notes an American emphasis on getting students to

express their thoughts, and she is happy that her children seem to like math more than they did in Japan. She is frustrated, though, that because of the lack of textbooks, she is not able to track and understand how her children are being taught.

Chinatsu makes an understandable but, in fact, incorrect assumption that all American children learn multiplication by drawing horizontal and vertical lines. This is one curricular approach among many, one that happened to have been chosen by the teacher or school district. Unlike Japan, where the available textbooks all use a similar approach, in the more individualistic, less homogeneous US, many approaches are accepted, and children learn multiplication in many different ways. This is just one of a multitude of ways individualism is conveyed as a value in the US.

Stories on a similar theme:

Some Educational Philosophy Differences (Education)

Make-up, Hair Styles and Clothes of Teenage Girls
Yumi Samura
Japan

Please read descriptions of:

Individualism and Collectivism
Homogeneity
Choice

Comment:

The long-standing value against centralized government control in the US makes many American parents reluctant to allow schools to dictate what their children will wear. Many US school districts do have some kind of minimal dress code, but these are fairly lenient compared to requiring identical school uniforms as in Japan. What

teens will wear (like what they will eat) seems, to many, to be
clearly in the personal domain.

In addition to this reluctance to let the government make decisions
is the primary value in the US on individualistic self-expression.
How one dresses is an obvious way to tell the world what kind of
person you are. Americans are particularly interested in helping
their children establish their identities as individuals. We tell them
to "be true to themselves," and to "stand out from the crowd." That
is harder if they are all wearing the same thing.

So, while in the past several years a few public school systems in
the US have adopted school uniforms, these are the exception.

Yumi is not, actually, particularly advocating school uniforms. She
thinks the regulation of clothing and appearance may have gone
too far in Japan. But she is also shocked by the American degree
of lenience. Yumi's social cohort is important to keep in mind here
– many of the parents at her child's high school were teenagers
during the 1960s and 1970s, and may be trying not to repeat the
struggles they had with their own parents over physical appearance. They may say to themselves, "Bell bottoms come and go.
Long hair, green hair, what's the difference?" Perhaps green hair is
different from wearing "lingerie," in terms of its effect on serious
study, but so far, the emphasis on individual expression is the more
important value in most American high schools.

Parent Involvement
Mayumi Toyoda
Japan

Please read descriptions of:

Power Distance
Homogeneity

Comment:

Mayumi's operating room metaphor emerged from the Club's discussion and seemed to the members to be an apt one. Deference to the professional teachers as a hands-off way of showing respect was an important value to the group. While US American parents respect teachers too, several factors contribute to a very different home-school relationship. First, US Americans' lower power distance makes both parents and teachers more comfortable with an egalitarian partnership in the education of each child. In addition, because Americans encourage teachers to be creative in their teaching and not to defer to a single national lesson plan, there is a wider range in approaches to teaching. Parents may be less likely to accept the notion of "leaving the teaching to the teachers." For their part, many US teachers appreciate the additional help of parents, both as curriculum enhancement and as a way of supporting the children's learning.

One way that parents become involved in a US classroom can be by offering to share a special skill or opportunity to one child's (usually one of their own children's) class. In the US system, one fourth-grade class visits a classmate's parent's glass blowing studio, while another class learns animation from another parent. Over time, Americans trust that these extra trips work out pretty evenly, at least within a school system. As these are all supplementary activities, US Americans are generally willing to trade a bit of equality for the enrichment opportunity. The commitment to decentralized control is evident – to US Americans it weighs even more than that prized value of equality. In discussing the issue of fairness when only one class gets exposed to a parent's special talents, Mayumi and others in the group said, "Yes, but in Japan, we believe in equality in education." Americans believe in equality in education too, but this story casts a bright light on how this belief plays out in different cultures.

Stories on a similar theme:

Parent Involvement, Grades and Modesty in School (Education)

Parent Involvement, Grades and Modesty in School
Kay (Ikei) Kobayashi
Japan

Please read descriptions of:

Power Distance
Formality and Informality
Harmony and Face
Modesty
Value Changes

Comment:

Here, Kay notes several distinct cultural differences in education. First, the low power distance she encounters in her US school feels odd to her. She is accustomed to a clear delineation (of power, influence, input) between "school" and "home," where parents do not feel invited or allowed to make suggestions, garner complaints, or otherwise be involved. Respect for teachers is enormous and unquestioned. While she appreciates the American opportunity to be involved in her children's education, the whole package does not feel quite natural to her. Specifically, when she contemplates adapting to the American practice of calling teachers by their first name, she feels torn between appearing too polite (if she does what feels more appropriate to her) and too rude (if she goes native).

The achievement level she hopes for in her children — 100% not 95% — is an excellent illustration of the difficulties parents face in raising bicultural children. In Japan, a persistent push for continuous improvement and excellence begins in childhood and is the norm in schools (and the workplace). Children grow up with feedback from teachers that focuses on their mistakes and how they could be doing better. Success in Japanese schools and admission to excellent universities in built within this system. In the US, educational goals revolve not only around attainment of specific knowledge, but also around developing life-long lovers of learning. Feeling good about oneself as a learner is therefore important, so effort is praised, successive approximations are acceptable, and...95% is considered excellent. Kay's children, raised exclusively in US schools, find her push for excellence a strain, and she is left feeling torn between cultures.

Similarly, she appreciates that her children are learning to express their opinions clearly and confidently. But...what about the value of being modest, humble, and deferential to those who know even more? She worries that they are missing out on these life skills and the ability to maintain harmonious relationships.

Stories on a similar theme:
How to React to Compliments (Communication)
Parent Involvement in Schools (Education)

School Lunch
Minako Maemura
Japan

Please read descriptions of:

Individualism and Collectivism
Choice
Homogeneity
Wastefulness

Comment:

Minako was struck by the difference in how the school lunch period
is handled in her home country vs. the US. For her, Japanese school
lunch time is an opportunity for learning – about nutrition, cooperation, hard work, thrift, gratitude – and a relief for mothers who
can trust that their children will be well fed. The US lunchroom
seems to her to be simply "time off" for the children and the teachers, a kind of free-for-all, nutritionally and behaviorally, with little
supervision about what the children eat or do with their uneaten
food. Lunch time is a refreshing break during a day of learning,
and a time to build social networks. The cultural values underlying
these two scenarios are profound.

Collectivist values are clearly reflected in this description of the
school lunch period. All the children eat the same portion of the
same meal, and the meals are prepared by other children. Team-
work and cooperation are taught in the process of preparing the
food. There is also a clear sense of work ethic instilled, as well as an
organized process which is respected and followed by all children
(the same way, in every school).

Many individualists, in general, resist others telling them what
to do, including what to eat. They tend to demand a lot of choice
and the right to avoid foods they don't like. Lunch time for them is

another moment to express one's individuality. Giving children a variety of food to choose from exercises their ability to think and decide for themselves at an early age. Although there are national guidelines about nutrition for federally-funded school lunches, there is relatively little attention paid to the quality and quantity of food consumed by individual children. Recent efforts to address the problem are motivated in part by the growing problem of obesity in the US.

Another point that Minako noted was the children's wastefulness – throwing away a half-eaten sandwich or untouched apple. Japan and the US have different histories with regard to plenitude and availability of resources. This story gives a wonderful example of how these values get transmitted from generation to generation. In Japan, a homeroom teacher supervises children finishing their lunch and not wasting anything; in the US, the lunch room monitor lets the food be tossed and the teachers, in the teacher's room on break, don't see it.

Stories on a similar theme:
Unnecessary Electricity (Customs)
The Culture of Dumping (Customs)
Clean Up Time (Education)

Self-Confidence
Mayumi Toyoda
Japan

Please read descriptions of:
Individualism and Collectivism
High vs. Low Context
Modesty
Communication Style

Comment:

Mayumi describes Americans' willingness to speak to the Reporter on the Street with admiration and surprise, and in doing so, highlights a cultural difference in values, expectations and communication style. She ties the difference to early school experiences in which children are encouraged to perform for others as individuals, highlighting one of the ways cultural differences in values, in this case, individualism-collectivism, are transmitted from generation to generation. Finally, Mayumi notes the difference in homogeneity between Japan and the US societies, as perhaps being at the root of this difference; here she is highlighting the high vs. low context nature of these two cultures. In high context cultures like Japan, she suggests, equality in educational experience is highly valued, and interpersonal understanding occurs easily because people's experience is so similar. Against this backdrop, a child's standing out, or performing for others, has a kind of unattractive show-off flavor. Mayumi's ability to accept and admire both cultures is a mark of her bicultural understanding.

Some Educational Philosophy Differences
Carolyn Yan
Taiwan

Please read descriptions of:
Individualism and Collectivism
Communication Style
Values Conflict

Comment:

Carolyn observes the cultural differences in US and Taiwanese classrooms with both a mother's and a teacher's eye. She offers a balanced assessment of the strengths and limitations of the US education philosophy – that promotes analysis and introspection at

the expense of drilling for proficiency, and that promotes, through
its small class size and teacher expectations, an accountability for
one's own learning and problem solving. One can hear Carolyn's dilemma in the last paragraph as she sees her daughter being a happy
learner, which she hopes will continue throughout her life, but worries that she is not learning as much as she would in Taiwan.

One of the differences that Carolyn notices is the American emphasis on getting students to express their thoughts, to make guesses
about how the world works, to solve problems for themselves, to
ask for individual help – in short, to use words to pursue their own
understanding and learning. American teachers are encouraging
their students to take control of and manage their own learning
(even though that means that they may not choose boring drills);
this is consistent with their goal of raising individualists to pursue
their own individual ends.

Stories on a similar theme:

Learning Math and How to Think (Customs)

Textbooks
Tomoko Shimizu
Japan

Please read descriptions of:

Individualism and Collectivism
Choice
Homogeneity

Comment:

There is a very strong preference in the US for leaving decisions to
local sites (states or towns) rather than the federal government unless there is some compelling and core value at stake. In fact, the US

196

Constitution specifically protects the rights of states to make many of their own laws. Many international newcomers are surprised at the laws that differ from state to state – from drivers' license laws to capital punishment.

The vast majority of decisions about education are among those that are not regulated by the US federal government. Teacher qualifications, graduation requirements, curriculum, number of days and hours of school, age of compulsory attendance, teaching method, and ... textbook choice – these all differ from state to state and, in some cases, from town to town or teacher to teacher.

So Tomoko is right when she notices the range in focus, style and quality of education across the country. Like the Japanese, Americans also believe in equality in education, but "local control" and "individuality" are strong competing values and so this commitment to "equality" ends up looking quite different.

The No Child Left Behind Act and recent federal educational initiatives have tried to bring oversight of some educational decisions back to the federal government, although even these laws leave the final educational decisions up to the states. The concept of a small number of textbooks chosen by the federal government to be used by all the children in a country is very foreign to the American ear. Americans like the idea of raising a country full of children who have learned very different things in very different ways.

Writing Letters Neatly
Kay (Ikei) Kobayashi
Japan

Please read descriptions of:
Individualism and Collectivism
Choice
Homogeneity

Comment:

American adults may remember handwriting classes and exercises from their school days, similar to what Kay describes, with an emphasis on posture, pencil holding, and feet-on-the-floor, too. For several reasons, though, the emphasis on good form and good output is different in the US compared to what Kay describes.

At a practical level, while today's teachers do have to teach handwriting, they also teach typing/keyboarding, including to quite young children. Some of the curricular time previously spent on handwriting form is thus displaced by this new technological literacy skill. (Presumably this has occurred in Japan, too.)

But a cultural dimension exists, too – even in the days when good handwriting was taught with more intensity in American schools, the assumption was that people would develop their own individual handwriting style that would be instantly identifiable. Large, small, slanted, loopy, round, flowery – from the basis of standard handwriting, these styles emerged for each student. In fact, some people practice "personality assessment" on the basis of a person's handwriting style. Thus, handwriting became one more way one's individuality could be expressed.

In Japan, in contrast, the goal is to match a standard style and maintain it, as a courtesy to the reader. Handwriting is not an opportunity for individuality, but rather a chance to demonstrate mastery of a classic style.

While handwriting may seem, at one level, to be a minor part of the educational curriculum, it is perhaps symbolic of a larger educational philosophical difference. On the one hand, a Japanese approach is to establish an ideal and emphasize mastery of it through structured learning. On the other hand, an American approach is to suggest a goal but allow a variety of routes and outcomes, valuing the diversity of output that follows from such an approach.

Dimension Descriptions

Communication Styles

People often make negative assumptions about people's motivation, politeness, sensitivity, competence, or integrity based on their communication style, when, in fact, the person is simply using a culturally-influenced style of communicating. It is important to understand these styles as a function of culture, to avoid making wrong assumptions about a person. Perhaps the most common cultural differences in communication style concern the communicators' level of verbal directness and confrontativeness. We think of these styles as falling along a continuum.

Direct/verbal communicators prefer to convey their messages in straightforward words, and speak them directly to each other. They tend to favor people putting their feelings into words and generally like explicit instructions about what people expect of them. They often prefer to resolve conflicts directly with those involved, even if that means that a conversation is a bit awkward. In general, they trust that the words they say are the most important thing, not the timing or the situation in which they say them. Direct/verbal communicators also tend not to rely on or perceive non-verbal cues to the same extent as indirect communicators

In contrast, indirect communicators prefer taking a more oblique approach, especially (but not only) when their message might be a difficult one. They prefer to communicate by making a suggestion or implication rather than a straightforward statement of intent or purpose. They prefer to resolve conflicts by finding ways to repair relationships and preserve face, even if the problem isn't completely solved. They might ask for a third party to convey a message rather than deliver it directly, if they feel this would minimize awkwardness. They tend to trust that a person's true meaning is best understood by his or her nonverbal behavior and the context of the situation, and may alter their interpretation of what someone says in light of their eye contact, timing, or other contextual factors.

When in disagreement with someone's ideas or work, confrontative communicators like to say so directly, verbally, since, after all, this is just a comment on their ideas, not on their integrity or competence. They see this style as important in being authentic and efficient.

In contrast, non-confrontative communicators try to find an indirect or gentle way of expressing disagreement. They worry about hurting the other's feelings, as they tend to see one's work and one's being as more intertwined. They see this style as important in being gentle and sensitive with others.

Interpersonal Boundaries

In every culture there is an established and agreed-upon invisible boundary between people, and between groups, which is taboo to invade. This can take a physical form – how close do you stand to someone when talking and how does it feel if someone invades the boundary and stands "too close?" But it can take a social form as well – do you make eye contact with, smile at, or talk to strangers? If you do chat with them, what kind of information is considered "too intimate" to share? When crossing cultures, one often encounters new rules about these boundaries and can break the rules unwittingly, with emotional consequences on both sides.

Individualism and Collectivism

According to Dutch interculturalist Geert Hofstede, no single society can be considered entirely individualistic or collectivistic, although most lean to one side of this continuum. A brief description of each is outlined below.

Individualism. In individualist societies, individual interests tend to prevail over group interests. Children in these societies are generally raised in nuclear families. They are taught to think for themselves and to have their own opinions and identities. "Standing out from the crowd" is a good thing, and parents are often proud of the ways in which their children are different from other children. As young adults, offspring are expected to move out of their parents' home. In these societies, people are only expected to take care of themselves and their immediate nuclear families. Self-reliance and independence, both socially and in one's thinking, are highly valued. It is generally considered unhealthy to be psychologically dependent on a group.

Collectivism. In collectivist societies, group interests prevail over individual interests. Children in these societies are more likely to be raised in extended families. The family structure differs slightly depending on the society, but generally consists of an extended family such as aunts, uncles, cousins, grandparents and, in some cases, servants, living closely together. One's membership and role in a group defines his/her identity. The in-group provides unconditional security and protection, and in return, its members owe the in-group absolute loyalty. Harmony and the interdependence of group members are highly valued. Toward this end, modesty is a highly valued trait. There is a mutual dependence, both psychologically and emotionally, among members of the group.

Power Distance

Power distance, as described by Geert Hofstede, is "the extent to which the less powerful members of organizations and institutions accept and expect that power is distributed unequally." While inequalities exist in most cultures, not all cultures accept this inequality as natural and inevitable.

High Power Distance. People in high power distance societies accept that inequalities in power and status are natural and inevitable. Just as they accept that some people are smarter, stronger, or more attractive, they also accept that some people have more power than others. In these societies, people with power generally try to distinguish themselves from those without it. They often call attention to their power and do not share or delegate it. They accept preferential treatment, demonstrations of subservience, and favors or benefits that result from their status. They are also expected to look after those who have less than they do. Individuals with less power are uncomfortable taking initiative or challenging their superiors' choices. They also willingly accept the preferential treatment shown to those with high power, and benefit from being the recipients of the care shown to them. People in high power distance cultures are generally quite aware and respectful of social hierarchies, including job status, age, etc.

Low Power Distance. People in low power distance societies believe that inequalities in power and status, while present in their culture, are to be fought against and squelched whenever possible. Those who do have more power or status tend to de-emphasize it, and often minimize differences between themselves and those with less power. They freely share and delegate power whenever possible, at least superficially and in many cases, actually. Those with less power are comfortable challenging and questioning the decisions made by their superiors. Low-power distance individuals generally do not like close supervision, as it reminds them of their one-down position, and are encouraged to take initiative.

Culture Shock Cycle

"Culture shock" takes many forms. Having an emotional reaction to moving to a new country is very normal, and in fact is often a signal that the person has moved beyond being a tourist and has begun the exciting journey of really living in a new culture. Still, it can be an unsettling and uncomfortable process. In many ways, "culture shock" is like a reaction to any other life transition or stress. People typically feel some combination of excitement and challenge that is part of the transition. While the timing and exact course differ from person to person, here is a typical course for a person to feel:

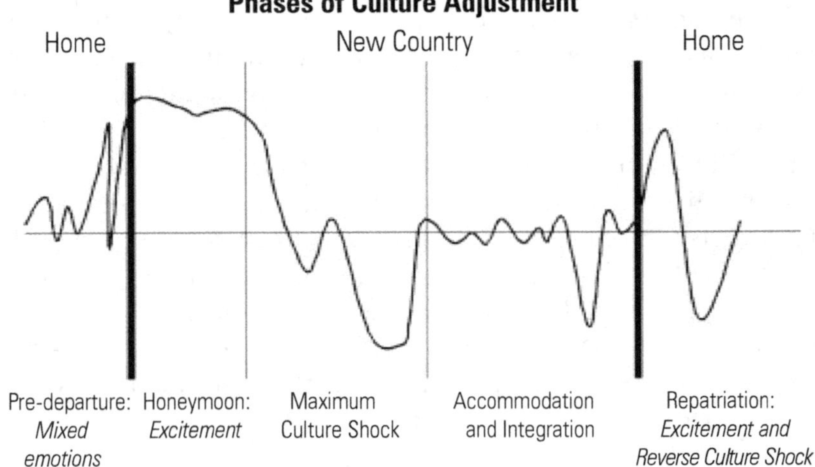

In the pre-departure period, it is common to feel alternately excited and overwhelmed by an international move. Expectations for a wonderful trip can be high, while managing the details of moving furniture, job, and family can be tiring. Then, upon arrival, many people experience a "honeymoon" period when they feel excited by all that is new — the food is exotic, everything looks picturesque, the people are friendly, optimism is high. This phase can last from a few days to a few months. After some time, usually when one stops being a tourist and begins really living in a new place, many (though not all) people begin to have "culture shock." Symptoms can include those that appear to be culture-related (anger at host nationals, homesickness), but also those that seem unrelated to the move (physical symptoms, fatigue, eating or sleeping changes). It is helpful to recognize all these signs as normal, expected reactions to living in a new culture; they usually diminish with time.

It is common for people then to enter a phase where they alternately feel pretty good and only fair. Of course, some people are uniformly happier on international assignment than at home; others are uniformly less happy. (See the section below on Value Changes for a description of some other kinds of changes, besides emotional ones, that occur during this period.)

206

Finally, along with a dip in adjustment around the time of departure, many people feel a surge of good feeling at the thought of moving (or even visiting) home. It is a surprise to many that they feel "reverse culture shock" - and a repeat of the symptoms felt early in the assignment. Returning home seems to challenge many people or a number of reasons. They may have adopted host national practices, values, clothes, attitudes, even without realizing it, and this may seem odd or foreign to them and those at home. They may have a new perspective on their home culture and may have a new view of world politics. They will have a new understanding of the many things that are culturally-influenced. People at home will also have changed with the years, though probably not in the same directions as the returnee has. This tends to widen the gap between them and their old friends. Many people are surprised that they feel like an outsider at home – it is one thing to feel like an outsider in a foreign country, but harder to feel like an outsider at home. And finally, people at home are generally unsympathetic with the repatriation challenge. It is hard to accept that going home is challenging, so they ignore the reasons for it.

Value Changes

Along with the excitement and stress of moving to another country comes the experience of understanding and adjusting to a new set of cultural values. Some of these adjustments are noticeable while living in a new country while others will only become apparent after the person has moved back to their host country and realizes how their values have changed. One of the gifts of living abroad is being able to see the world in a different way. Individuals and families discover that values they thought were universal are in fact not. As views and understanding of cultural values begin to expand, individuals and families may find some of their own value preferences beginning to shift and evolve. Some of the values of the host country will be appreciated and adopted immediately; some may be incorporated over time; and others may clash too drastically with existing values and therefore never be accepted into the individuals value system. Whatever the case may be, people who move to a new country and culture will find their view of the world broadened to acknowledge an entirely new set of values.

One clear model for capturing the possibilities for value changes has been offered by John Berry. Those who live in and know two cultures (for example, expatriates and immigrants and their children and grandchildren) may choose to have a lot of contact with the new culture (or not) and may choose to maintain their home-country cultural values and habits (or not). Berry proposes a 2x2 set of possibilities:

<table>
<tr><td colspan="2" rowspan="2"></td><td colspan="2">Berry Model of Acculturation
Cultural Maintenance</td></tr>
<tr><td>Yes</td><td>No</td></tr>
<tr><td rowspan="2">Contact Participation</td><td>Yes</td><td>Integration: want to maintain their identity with their home culture, but also want to take on some characteristics of the new culture</td><td>Assimilation: do not want to keep their identity from their home culture, but would rather take on the characteristics of the new culture</td></tr>
<tr><td>No</td><td>Separation/Segregation: want to separate themselves from the new culture; if this separation is forced rather than chosen, the term "segregation" is used</td><td>Marginalization: do not want anything to do with either the new culture or the old culture.</td></tr>
</table>

Burdening Others

The themes of obligation and burden are prevalent in both individualist and collectivist societies but the way these concepts are perceived differs. The motivation for self-reliant behavior differs between the two ends of this cultural dimension. The focus of self-reliance in collectivist societies is on not burdening others while in individualist societies, self-reliance is important as a marker of independence. So while individualists strive for self-reliance to avoid being indebted or feeling an obligation towards someone else, collectivists maintain a cycle of reciprocity where burdens and obligations are constantly being negotiated back and forth

High vs. Low Context

Not all cultures communicate in the same manner. One significant difference is to what extent context is used to provide meaning during communications. In his 1976 book, *Beyond Culture,* Edward T. Hall presented the concept of *high* and *low context communication.* All cultures use a variety of high context or low context styles of communication, but the situations and frequency with which these modes of communication are used will vary.

High Context. In high context communication, meaning is conveyed through the context of a situation, through shared histories and understandings. Less emphasis is placed on explicit verbal communication. Meaning is implicit rather than explicit. Verbal and non-verbal communications are interpreted through a shared history and experiences, rather than the literal interpretation of what is explicitly stated. High context communication may be more prevalent in collectivist cultures where in-groups are more tightly knit, creating a strong shared history of understanding and meaning. An example of high context communication that exists in most cultures could be a married couple of 30 years who can communicate volumes with just a look or a word because of a long shared history. High context environments can be difficult to enter as an outsider because much of what is communicated is "below the surface," a type of "communication short hand" that depends on extensive knowledge of the in-group.

Low Context. Low context communication relies more on a literal interpretation of what is explicitly stated. Meaning is embedded in written language or verbal communication moreso than the situational context. Low context situations are fairly easy to enter because information is explicitly stated rather than interpreted. In low context communications you "say what you mean and mean what you say." Knowledge tends to be public, external and accessible to everyone.

Choice

One result of living in an individualistic, low-context culture in which people have an enhanced sense of control over their own lives (like the US) is a preponderance of choice, in virtually every aspect of life. Raised to be assertive about one's own individual wants (as individualists), to articulate these wants explicitly (as is done in a low-context culture), and to believe that life's outcome, in general, is controllable, US Americans find it natural to demand and expect plenty of choice – in how their food will be served in a restaurant, in how many options will be available in a supermarket, in where and when to take a vacation, etc. US American parents also tend to give their children more choices than those from many other cultures — for example, about what food to eat, what friends to have, what sports to play, and what career path to follow. In many other cultures, these decisions are made by an elder or parent rather than by the child.

Effort Optimism

In survey after survey, US Americans score among the highest in the world in the belief that they have control over their own lives – that they are the captains of their own fate, that what happens to them is their own doing, and that probably things will work out well if they try hard enough. This effort optimism, which has an underlying orientation towards the future, is a deeply held value that undoubtedly has had a positive impact on productivity, resilience and innovation, but may also have had unintended social and emotional implication. If you believe that if something good happens to you it is because you did something right, then you are likely to believe the converse, too – that if something bad happens it is because you did something wrong. Effort optimists generally believe that hard work is rewarded by success, and that with enough determination any goal can be reached. They are also more likely to blame those with less status in a society and tend not to cope well with natural tragedy or disaster.

Homogeneity

One result of living in a collectivist, high-context culture is that a consensus can develop about the "best" way to teach, or the "best" way to live one's life. A value is placed on fitting in smoothly and seamlessly, and on knowing how to behave without explicit instructions. The more people are treated the same (e.g. taught using the same textbooks, hear news from the same source, have the same job), the more they, naturally, begin to have similar ideas. To high-context collectivists, homogeneity is often a preferred outcome because it demonstrates evidence of equality of opportunity and is predictive of smooth relations. Conversely, in societies that fall on the individualist, low-context end of the spectrum, heterogeneity is preferred and individuals and organizations are often encouraged to stand out from the crowd and express their own unique identities.

Harmony and Face

An important feature of collectivist cultures is their emphasis on smooth – harmonious – interpersonal relationships. The ensuing belief is that where there is a well-functioning group, there will be productivity and success. In this context, a "well-functioning" group is one in which people are careful not to let anyone else lose face (be shown to have made a mistake and therefore feel ashamed). Communication styles tend to be indirect, non-verbal and non-confrontative, as these are ones that are likely to instill a sense of harmony into the group.

Modesty

A value related to collectivism and harmony/face is the value of modesty – deflecting attention away from oneself, sharing credit or rewards with others, minimizing individual contribution in deference to others. Where the group's identity and success are critical (to a project's success, or to a family's status or well-being), it is not becoming or admired to attract, or even accept, individual praise or attention. A Japanese proverb says, "The nail that sticks out gets pounded down." Note the profound difference between that and individualistic proverbs (like "The squeaky wheel gets the grease" or admonitions (like "Shine like a star" or "Grab you time in the sun.")

Wastefulness

A lack of consciousness about the environment and the consequences of wasting resources is more possible in a large country with lots of open space (like the US) than in a small peninsula or island countries with little undeveloped land (like Japan, Korea and Taiwan). From the pioneer days of the nineteenth century, Americans developed an attitude of vast plenitude, where more good fertile land seemed available to anyone willing to move a bit further west. Americans have not had the immediate motivation to solve the problem of resource usage in the way many other nations have. An environmental motivation — that being careful of the earth's resources is necessary for the sake of the planet — has been harder to impress on people in US, as it runs counter to the deeply held belief that there is plenty to go around.

Appendix

The International Writers' Club: Ours and Yours
By Anne P. Copeland

A number of years ago, as I registered my daughter for kindergarten at our neighborhood primary public school, I was delighted to learn that the student body would be 30% international, and even higher in the lower grades. Because of a Japanese language support program at that school, many of the international students in the lower grades would be Japanese, but there would be dozens of different passports represented among the 450 students. (Other schools in the system provide similar support for other major language groups.) Having just returned from a sojourn abroad, and being well-acquainted with the limits of growing up in a wholly homogeneous world, I was eager for my children to be raised in a culturally diverse environment.

I eagerly jumped into the available international activities at the school. I joined the International Mothers' Club (a Friday-night social group), organized a host family exchange, shopped enthusiastically at the annual Japanese food fair, and learned to make some cool earrings at Origami Night.

But I was struck by how few of my American peers seemed interested in the opportunity that our international environment provided. When I sought out host families for my exchange program, I heard things like: "It's so hard when they don't speak English," "I'm afraid I'll serve the wrong food and it'll be embarrassing," "There's all that nodding and smiling but no real conversation," and "They're just going to be here a few years; what's the point?"

How to go beyond Origami Night? What could be done to surmount the very real impediments to having solid intercultural relationships, and to entice intercultural interaction that would, itself, reveal the inherent benefits and insights that come from beginning to understand another culture?

The mother of my daughter's [Japanese] best friend, came up with

the solution: an English-learning-focused Writers' Club that meets
during school hours when the [mostly not-currently-employed] Japanese mothers would be freer of family obligations.

How the Club Works. For each meeting, two or three people write
a short essay about some cultural difference they have observed
while living in the US. They explain what they have seen, how it differs from home, and what they would like Americans to understand
about the difference. I offer English editing comments, then send the
"corrected" copy around to the rest of the Club members. We meet in
my home, and discuss the essays and the cultural values they reveal.

One note about the editing: At the writers' request, I edit every essay
to correct grammar, syntax and vocabulary errors. Part of their motivation for coming to the Club is to improve their English, and they
feel better about having their essays distributed among Club members and the school community if they do not have to worry about
having made mistakes. My challenge has been to offer this instruction in English without removing their voice altogether. My guiding
rule has been to make each sentence grammatically correct, but not
necessarily colloquial.

Who Are the Writers? We invited anyone in the school community
who was interested in exploring cultural differences to join the Club.
At first, the group included mostly Japanese, a few Americans and a
few Europeans. One year I co-led the group with a colleague connected to the Korean-support school in our town, so we soon had a good
number of Koreans, too. Through word of mouth, we got connected
to a Taiwanese network, and so over time, although it remained (and
remains) open to all, the great bulk of essays (and all those included
in this collection) are from Japanese, Korean or Taiwanese writers.

Most of the members of Club are/were in the US temporarily, for
reasons having to do with their spouse's work. This is in contrast to
many other international communities, including some in my town,
where international newcomers tend to be immigrants, here permanently. A number of factors shaped this specific situation. They
tended to have come for short-term fellowships or degree programs

at the medical or university centers nearby, with plans and/or contracts to return home at the completion of their program. The Japanese, Korean and Taiwanese economies generally drew this group
of professionals back to their homes. And, while living in the US was
clearly a desirable choice for them, staying "too long" would make
it difficult for their children to re-adjust. So, for the most part, these
writers were exploring the experience of living in the US temporarily,
with an eye toward returning home in the relatively near future. This
surely affected their experience, hopes, and observations. We get a
glimpse of the immigrants' experiences from several of the essays by
writers whose plans changed and are now in the US indefinitely.

I adopted the practice of calling Club members by their given names,
US style ("Minako" rather than "Maemura-san"). This was the norm
in our school, and the members graciously accept it as a US custom.
We have continued that practice in the Comments in this collection.

What are the Benefits of the Club? The obvious benefits are to
the members who get practice writing and speaking English, and
a chance to discuss their experience with others walking a similar
path, with a guide who has the vocabulary to label some of the sites
they pass along the way.

But the school community also directly benefits: as it happened, I
was the Editor of the school newsletter at the time the Club began.
With the Club members' permission, I published the essays, along
with a short intercultural framing of the issues, in each school newsletter. The writers were happy to have a voice in this community, and
the American parents and teachers loved the essays and the chance
to hear the experience of this part of their community.

I consider the Club to be part English class, part support group, part
cross-cultural training, and part primary prevention. And with the
publication of this collection, the Club has taken on a role in "product
development" for those living and working in multi-cultural environments seeking to understand how the world looks to their new
neighbors.

If You Want to Start Your Own Writers' Club

Our International Writers' Club sits in a unique time and place, as described above, and it is impossible to know just what aspects of it have been important to its success. Here are a number of factors that certainly shaped the Club's course:

Clear Personal and Institutional Context. From the beginning, there was a clear understanding among Club members just where this Club "fit" in their community – it was an adaptation of a previous school activity with known participants, and was introduced by a trusted Japanese mother who had been involved in the school for several years. While a volunteer, non-school-sponsored activity, it was announced in the English and Japanese school newsletter and so sat within that context. Newcomers understandably question what are "legitimate" groups and look for such signs of institutional and personal connection. Further, some combination of word-of-mouth and a sense of responsibility among the members to ensure that "enough people show up for each meeting" safeguarded continuity in the face of a rather transitory population.

Critical Mass of Several Nationalities. For a host of reasons, including the structure of this school system's language support programs (with each school specializing in one language), this Club tended to draw members from three particular nationalities – Japanese, Korean and Taiwanese. This gave members the chance to compare notes within their own cultural experience and with their geographic neighbors. A more varied Club membership would have brought different strengths, of a wider diversity of perspectives, but might not have felt as cohesive.

Training of Facilitator. Anne Copeland wore three hats during each meeting: that of clinical psychologist, interculturalist, and mother peer. Each of these roles brought their own credibility and skills – knowledge of the psychological processes and stresses involved in intercultural transition, familiarity with American educational values, a vocabulary for discussing members' common expatriate cultural course and the cultural differences they encountered, practice in

216

speaking to non-native English speakers, and the shared experience as a mother in this particular school community.

Commitment of Writers to Write Respectfully. Finally, the major credit goes to the Club members themselves, for their remarkable ability to reflect thoughtfully about the cultural differences they encountered, and to write about their observations in a non-accusatory and non-defensive way. They have, we believe, encouraged their readers to want to hear more from them.

If you decide to start your own Writers' Club, we would love to hear about your experience – what you did differently, what worked and what didn't, and what you've learned: Please write to us at writers@ interchangeinstitute.org. We will facilitate an on-line dialogue among all who are trying this approach.

Indexes

Stories By Country of Author

Japan

221

Stories By
Illustrated Dimension

Burdening Others:

Choice

Communication Style

Culture Shock Cycle

Effort Optimism

224

Interpersonal Boundaries

Modesty

Power Distance

Value Changes

Wastefulness

About the Authors

Dr. Anne P. Copeland is a clinical psychologist and the founder and Executive Director of The Interchange Institute. She has done extensive research on the process of moving to a new country, with a particular focus on the experiences of accompanying spouses and children. She writes books and newsletters and conducts cross-cultural training workshops for people moving into and out of the US. Her training-of-trainers workshop, *Crossing Cultures with Competence*, has prepared hundreds of intercultural professionals around the world to develop and offer top-quality cultural orientations. Prior to founding The Interchange Institute, Dr. Copeland was Associate Professor in the Psychology Department at Boston University. She lives in Brookline, Massachusetts.

Dr. Marissa R. Lombardi is the Dean of Students at Lorenzo de' Medici International Institute, a higher education Institute for foreigners in Florence, Italy. She also teaches in Northeastern University's Master's in International Affairs and Global Studies program. Her research interests include intercultural transition, intercultural competence development and internationalization in higher education. She also specializes in cross-cultural training. She holds a Master of Arts in intercultural relations from Lesley University and a doctorate in education from Northeastern University. Previously, she taught in the Global Studies Department at Bentley University and also directed an English language and culture program at an Arab bank in Rome, Italy. She lives in Florence, Italy.

About The Interchange Institute

The Interchange Institute is a not-for-profit research and educational institution focused on the needs of people who move from one country to another. Its research focuses on the impact of intercultural transitions on individuals and families. From the results of this research, the Institute provides training workshops, books and newsletters. Its publications include:

Newcomer's Almanac: A Newsletter for Newcomers to the United States
Understanding American Schools: The Answers to Newcomers' Most Frequently Asked Questions
Hello! USA
A Smooth Beginning: 20 Suggestions to Help Your Family Feel Settled in a New Country
Global Baby: Tips to Keep You and Your Infant Smiling Before, During and After Your International Move

See www.interchangeinstitute.org for more information.